Barbara Jo Brothers
Editor

The Abuse of Men:
Trauma Begets Trauma

The Abuse of Men: Trauma Begets Trauma has been co-published simultaneously as *Journal of Couples Therapy*, Volume 10, Number 1 2001.

Pre-Publication
REVIEWS,
COMMENTARIES,
EVALUATIONS . . .

"This edited volume addresses a topic that has been neglected in the literature: the abuse of men. It is unique in adopting a systemic perspective that focuses not solely on the males who have been abused but also on their partners and family members. The contributors convincingly argue that effective treatment must include not only the male survivor but also his spouse, partner, or other family members, because everyone intimately connected to the survivor will also have to cope with the effects of the trauma in order for healing to take place. This volume will be of greatest interest to new clinicians who are looking for direction for intervening with the population of abused males, their partners, and their families. Most helpful will be the final chapter which gives detailed and specific directions for intervening with couples who have experienced multiple traumas."

Joseph A. Micucci, PhD
Associate Professor of Psychology
Chestnut Hill College
Pennsylvania

"**O**ne of the major strengths of this book is the multidimensional examination of the abuse of men. Of particular note is the attention given to the trauma associated with men being abused, couple stress, systemic factors relating to abuse, and the secondary traumatic stress affecting men whose partners were sexually abused. The contributors to this book offer a compelling call for an examination of personal and professional issues relating to men as both victims and perpetrators of abuse. Through case study, personal narrative, and a review of research this informative book will undoubtedly promote discussion among practitioners, educators, and researchers concerned with family violence and couples."

Nicholas Mazza, PhD
Professor of Social Work
Florida State University, Tallahassee

The Haworth Press, Inc.

The Abuse of Men:
Trauma Begets Trauma

The Abuse of Men: Trauma Begets Trauma has been co-published simultaneously as *Journal of Couples Therapy*, Volume 10, Number 1 2001.

The Journal of Couples Therapy Monographic "Separates"

Below is a list of "separates," which in serials librarianship means a special issue simultaneously published as a special journal issue or double-issue and as a "separate" hardbound monograph. (This is a format which we also call a "DocuSerial.")

"Separates" are published because specialized libraries or professionals may wish to purchase a specific thematic issue by itself in a format which can be separately cataloged and shelved, as opposed to purchasing the journal on an on-going basis. Faculty members may also more easily consider a "separate" for classroom adoption.

"Separates" are carefully classified separately with the major book jobbers so that the journal tie-in can be noted on new book order slips to avoid duplicate purchasing.

You may wish to visit Haworth's website at . . .

http://www.HaworthPress.com

. . . to search our online catalog for complete tables of contents of these separates and related publications.

You may also call 1-800-HAWORTH (outside US/Canada: 607-722-5857), or Fax 1-800-895-0582 (outside US/Canada: 607-771-0012), or e-mail at:

getinfo@haworthpressinc.com

The Abuse of Men: Trauma Begets Trauma, edited by Barbara Jo Brothers, MSW, BCSW (Vol. 10, No. 1, 2001). *"Addresses a topic that has been neglected. . . . This book is unique in adopting a systemic perspective that focuses not solely on the males who have been abused but also on their partners and family members. . . . Gives detailed and specific directions for intervening with couples who have experienced multiple traumas." (Joseph A. Micucci, PhD, Associate Professor of Psychology, Chestnut Hill College, Pennsylvania)*

The Personhood of the Therapist, edited by Barbara Jo Brothers, MSW, BCSW (Vol. 9, No. 3/4, 2000). *Through suggestions, techniques, examples, and case studies, this book will help you develop a great sense of openness about yourself and your feelings, enabling you to offer clients more effective services.*

Couples Connecting: Prerequisites of Intimacy, edited by Barbara Jo Brothers, MSW, BCSW (Vol. 9, No. 1/2, 2000). *"Brothers views marriage as an ideal context for the psychological and spiritual evolution of human beings, and invites therapists to reflect on the role they can play in facilitating this. Readers are sure to recognize their clients among the examples given and to return to their work with a renewed vision of the possibilities for growth and change." (Eleanor D. Macklin, PhD, Emeritus Professor and former Director of the Marriage and Family Therapy program, Syracuse University, New York)*

Couples Therapy in Managed Care: Facing the Crisis, edited by Barbara Jo Brothers, MSW, BCSW (Vol. 8, No. 3/4, 1999). *Provides social workers, psychologists, and counselors with an overview of the negative effects of the managed care industry on the quality of mental health care. Within this book, you will discover the paradoxes that occur with the mixing of business principles and service principles and find valuable suggestions on how you can creatively cope within the managed care context. With* Couples Therapy in Managed Care, *you will learn how you can remain true to your own integrity and still get paid for your work and offer quality services within the current context of managed care.*

Couples and Pregnancy: Welcome, Unwelcome, and In-Between, edited by Barbara Jo Brothers, MSW, BCSW (Vol. 8, No. 2, 1999). *Gain valuable insight into how pregnancy and birth have a profound psychological effect on the parents' relationship, especially on their experience of intimacy.*

Couples, Trauma, and Catastrophes, edited by Barbara Jo Brothers, MSW, BCSW (Vol. 7, No. 4, 1998). *Helps therapists and counselors working with couples facing major crises and trauma.*

Couples: A Medley of Models, edited by Barbara Jo Brothers, MSW, BCSW, BCD (Vol. 7, No. 2/3, 1998). *"A wonderful set of authors who illuminate different corners of relationships. This book belongs on your shelf . . . but only after you've read it and loved it."* (Derek Paar, PhD, Associate Professor of Psychology, Springfield College, Massachusetts)

When One Partner Is Willing and the Other Is Not, edited by Barbara Jo Brothers, MSW (Vol. 7, No. 1, 1997). *"An engaging variety of insightful perspectives on resistance in couples therapy."* (Stan Taubman, DSW, Director of Managed Care, Alameda County Behavioral Health Care Service, Berkeley, California; Author, Ending the Struggle Against Yourself)

Couples and the Tao of Congruence, edited by Barbara Jo Brothers, MSW, BCSW (Vol. 6, No. 3/4, 1996). *"A library of information linking Virginia Satir's teaching and practice of creative improvement in human relations and the Tao of Congruence. . . . A stimulating reader."* (Josephine A. Bates, DSW, BD, retired mental health researcher and family counselor, Lake Preston, South Dakota)

Couples and Change, edited by Barbara Jo Brothers, MSW, BCSW (Vol. 6, No. 1/2, 1996). *This enlightening book presents readers with Satir's observations–observations that show the difference between thinking with systems in mind and thinking linearly–of process, interrelatedness, and attitudes.*

Couples: Building Bridges, edited by Barbara Jo Brothers, MSW, BCSW (Vol. 5, No. 4, 1996). *"This work should be included in the library of anyone considering to be a therapist or who is one or who is fascinated by the terminology and conceptualizations which the study of marriage utilizes."* (Irv Loev, PhD, MSW-ACP, LPC, LMFT, private practitioner)

Couples and Countertransference, edited by Barbara Jo Brothers, MSW, BCSW (Vol. 5, No. 3, 1995). *"I would recommend this book to beginning and advanced couple therapists as well as to social workers and psychologists. . . . This book is a wealth of information."* (International Transactional Analysis Association)

Power and Partnering, edited by Barbara Jo Brothers, MSW, BCSW (Vol. 5, No. 1/2, 1995). *"Appeals to therapists and lay people who find themselves drawn to the works of Virginia Satir and Carl Jung. Includes stories and research data satisfying the tastes of both left- and right-brained readers."* (Virginia O. Felder, ThM, Licensed Marriage and Family Therapist, private practice, Atlanta, Georgia)

Surpassing Threats and Rewards: Newer Plateaus for Couples and Coupling, edited by Barbara Jo Brothers, MSW, BCSW (Vol. 4, No. 3/4, 1995). *Explores the dynamics of discord, rejection, and blame in the coupling process and provides practical information to help readers understand marital dissatisfaction and how this dissatisfaction manifests itself in relationships.*

Attraction and Attachment: Understanding Styles of Relationships, edited by Barbara Jo Brothers, MSW, BCSW (Vol. 4, No. 1/2, 1994). *"Ideas on working effectively with couples. . . . I strongly recommend this book for those who want to have a better understanding of the complex dynamics of couples and couples therapy."* (Gilbert J. Greene, PhD, ACSW, Associate Professor, College of Social Work, The Ohio State University)

Peace, War, and Mental Health: Couples Therapists Look at the Dynamics, edited by Barbara Jo Brothers, MSW, BCSW (Vol. 3, No. 4, 1993). *Discover how issues of world war and peace relate to the dynamics of couples therapy in this thought-provoking book.*

Couples Therapy, Multiple Perspectives: In Search of Universal Threads, edited by Barbara Jo Brothers, MSW, BCSW (Vol. 3, No. 2/3, 1993). *"A very sizeable team of couples therapists has scoured the countryside in search of the most effective methods for helping couples improve their relationships. . . . The bibliographies are a treasury of worthwhile references."* (John F. Sullivan, EdS, Marriage and Family Counselor in Private Practice, Newburgh, New York)

Spirituality and Couples: Heart and Soul in the Therapy Process, edited by Barbara Jo Brothers, MSW, BCSW (Vol. 3, No. 1, 1993). *"Provides an array of reflections particularly for therapists beginning to address spirituality in the therapeutic process."* (Journal of Family Psychotherapy)

Equal Partnering: A Feminine Perspective, edited by Barbara Jo Brothers, MSW, BCSW (Vol. 2, No. 4, 1992). *Designed to help couples, married or not, understand how to achieve a balanced, equal partnership.*

Coupling . . . What Makes Permanence? edited by Barbara Jo Brothers, MSW, BCSW (Vol. 2, No. 3, 1991). *"Explores what it is that makes for a relationship in which each partner can grow and develop while remaining attached to another." (The British Journal of Psychiatry)*

Virginia Satir: Foundational Ideas, edited by Barbara Jo Brothers, MSW, BCSW (Vol. 2, No. 1/2, 1991). *"The most thorough conglomeration of her ideas available today. Done in the intimate, yet clear fashion you would expect from Satir herself. . . . Well worth getting your hands damp to pick up this unique collection." (Journal of Family Psychotherapy)*

Intimate Autonomy: Autonomous Intimacy, edited by Barbara Jo Brothers, MSW, BCSW (Vol. 1, No. 3/4, 1991). *"A fine collection of chapters on one of the most difficult of human tasks–getting close enough to another to share the warmth and benefits of that closeness without losing what is precious in our separations." (Howard Halpern, PhD, Author,* How to Break Your Addiction to a Person*)*

Couples on Coupling, edited by Barbara Jo Brothers, MSW, BCSW (Vol. 1, No. 2, 1990). *"A variety of lenses through which to view relationships, each providing a different angle for seeing patterns, strengths, and problems and for gaining insight into a given couple system." (Suzanne Imes, PhD, Clinical Psychologist, Private Practice, Atlanta, Georgia; Adjunct Assistant Professor of Psychology, Georgia State University)*

The Abuse of Men:
Trauma Begets Trauma

Barbara Jo Brothers
Editor

The Abuse of Men: Trauma Begets Trauma has been co-published simultaneously as *Journal of Couples Therapy*, Volume 10, Number 1 2001.

The Haworth Press, Inc.
New York • London • Oxford

The Abuse of Men: Trauma Begets Trauma has been co-published simultaneously as *Journal of Couples Therapy*, Volume 10, Number 1 2001.

The development, preparation, and publication of this work has been undertaken with great care. However, the publisher, employees, editors, and agents of The Haworth Press and all imprints of The Haworth Press, Inc., including The Haworth Medical Press® and Pharmaceutical Products Press®, are not responsible for any errors contained herein or for consequences that may ensue from use of materials or information contained in this work. Opinions expressed by the author(s) are not necessarily those of The Haworth Press, Inc.

The Haworth Press, Inc., 10 Alice Street, Binghamton, NY 13904-1580 USA

Cover design by Thomas J. Mayshock Jr.

Library of Congress Cataloging-in-Publication Data

The abuse of men: trauma begets trauma/Barbara Jo Brothers, editor.
     p. cm.
     ". . . has been co-published simultaneously as Journal of couples therapy, volume 10, number 1, 2001"
     Includes bibliographical references and index.
     ISBN 0-7890-1378-9 (alk. paper)–ISBN 0-7890-1379-7 (alk. paper)
     1. Abused men. 2. Adult child abuse victims. 3. Husband abuse. 4. Psychic trauma. 5. Psychotherapy. I. Brothers, Barbara Jo, 1940- II. Journal of couples therapy.

HV1441.4.A28 2001
362.8–dc21

2001024317

Indexing, Abstracting & Website/Internet Coverage

This section provides you with a list of major indexing & abstracting services. That is to say, each service began covering this periodical during the year noted in the right column. Most Websites which are listed below have indicated that they will either post, disseminate, compile, archive, cite or alert their own Website users with research-based content from this work. (This list is as current as the copyright date of this publication.)

Special Bibliographic Notes related to special journal issues
(separates) and indexing/abstracting:

- indexing/abstracting services in this list will also cover material in any "separate" that is co-published simultaneously with Haworth's special thematic journal issue or DocuSerial. Indexing/abstracting usually covers material at the article/chapter level.
- monographic co-editions are intended for either non-subscribers or libraries which intend to purchase a second copy for their circulating collections.
- monographic co-editions are reported to all jobbers/wholesalers/approval plans. The source journal is listed as the "series" to assist the prevention of duplicate purchasing in the same manner utilized for books-in-series.
- to facilitate user/access services all indexing/abstracting services are encouraged to utilize the co-indexing entry note indicated at the bottom of the first page of each article/chapter/contribution.
- this is intended to assist a library user of any reference tool (whether print, electronic, online, or CD-ROM) to locate the monographic version if the library has purchased this version but not a subscription to the source journal.
- individual articles/chapters in any Haworth publication are also available through the Haworth Document Delivery Service (HDDS).

The Abuse of Men: Trauma Begets Trauma

CONTENTS

ABOUT THE EDITOR

Barbara Jo Brothers, MSW, BCD, a Diplomate in Clinical Social Work, National Association of Social Workers, is in private practice in New Orleans. She received her BA from the University of Texas and her MSW from Tulane University, where she is currently on the faculty. She was Editor of *The Newsletter of the American Academy of Psychotherapists* from 1976 to 1985, and was Associate Editor of *Voices: The Art and Science of Psychotherapy* from 1979 to 1989. She has 30 years of experience, in both the public and private sectors, helping people to form skills that will enable them to connect emotionally. The author of numerous articles and book chapters on authenticity in human relating, she has advocated healthy, congruent communication that builds intimacy as opposed to destructive, incongruent communication which blocks intimacy. In addition to her many years of direct work with couples and families, Ms. Brothers has led numerous workshops on teaching communication in families and has also played an integral role in the development of training programs in family therapy for mental health workers throughout the Louisiana state mental health system. She is a board member of the Institute for International Connections, a non-profit organization for cross-cultural professional development focused on training and cross-cultural exchange with psychotherapists in Russia, republics once part of what used to be the Soviet Union, and other Eastern European countries.

Models of Perceiving the World: Relationship as Hierarchy

Virginia Satir

EDITOR'S NOTE. The following lectures were part of Virginia Satir's month long training seminar in Crested Butte, Colorado, Process Community I, August 1981 and Process Community III, 1983. The lectures would take place before and after demonstrations, communication exercises, centering exercises, and role playing. The reader must take into consideration this is the transcription of words being spoken to a live audience.

One of the things you will know if you have much to do with me is that I move back and forth between metaphor, analogy, and fact. What's interesting, too, is that many times the metaphor becomes fact later. . . .

. . . I have all kinds of experiences, and then at a certain point I stand back and I say to myself, "What is this? It's moving up and down and this thing comes in and out all the time." And I have to give myself that space to look at what's going on, because when I'm busy doing it, I can't look at myself doing it. Have you ever noticed that about yourself? When you take videotapes of yourself don't you sometimes look funny? I know I do. You're so busy doing what you do you can't step back.

Now over the length of time I've told you I've been in the professional world, I noticed something. I noticed that there are four phenomena, four phenomena that–if I understood how people perceived these phenomena and how they lived and communicated them–I would understand practically everything about them. That's a very

[Haworth co-indexing entry note]: "Models of Perceiving the World: Relationship as Hierarchy." Satir, Virginia. Co-published simultaneously in *Journal of Couples Therapy* (The Haworth Press, Inc.) Vol. 10, No. 1, 2001, pp. 1-8; and: *The Abuse of Men: Trauma Begets Trauma* (ed: Barbara Jo Brothers) The Haworth Press, Inc., 2001, pp. 1-8.

strong statement, [but] you'll see how everything fits. It is, in a way, similar to a physician who finds out how all the body parts are hung together. In any body, he can be pretty sure that he's going to find the lungs right behind here [gesturing toward chest]. They don't usually flop down at the bottom.

So these four phenomena have to do with all people and their interrelationship with one another, and I mean to leave no people out. No religion, no nationality, no age, no professional group, none. No males or females either.

DEFINITION OF A RELATIONSHIP

These four phenomena had to do, first of all, with how I *define a relationship*. In other words, how do I see a pair, how do I describe it? I'm using relationship now as a moment in time, a dyad or a pair. Dyad is the fancy name, pair the usual.

You've noticed, no doubt, that you're not fish. Many fish have eyes on *each* side of their head . . . If you had eyes on each side of your head you could see everything over *here* and what's over *there*. But we humans are limited because we have to have our eyes in focus at one point or we can't see anything. So that the only place that we can be completely focused in relationship is on one other person at a time. Try it. Even if you've got astigmatism it won't change.

So, this is what I call a relationship. You can shift, of course, because you can move . . . you can shift but never can I just half look at you. That's the way people get dizzy.

The second phenomenon has to do with the *definition of a person*. How do you define a person? We live by this definition we give a person, because that's how we limit or extend ourselves.

Then the third one is *how we explain events,* the why of something. Why did this happen? Why did you wear out your shoe on the left side rather than the right side? That's an event, your shoe wore out. So why did you? We have this fantastic left brain, that's always saying, "My, why does the sun not set there?" And if you listen to little children, they will ask all these beautiful questions that you can't answer. And that's how we start out getting silly answers in childhood, because we ask questions that are really questions that nobody can answer.

Then the last one has to do with *attitude toward change.*

Every once in a while, I smile because people talk as though change is something that they legislate. It's so funny . . . [No.] Change is constant. There is no such thing as "we can wait for change." There's no such thing. So, in this event, what is the attitude toward change?

I'm going to show you first the things I see on one level of all this. I think I have worked in every conceivable place where people come with human problems. Mental hospitals, prisons, schools, clinics, residential treatment center . . . whether it was schizophrenia, or a cancer problem [in] which I was helping some physician who was working on it, or whether it was a non-learning problem or dyslexia or delinquency, it doesn't matter. I got a chance at all of them. And the interesting thing is I found the same things operating. The method of growing is the same, whether the flower is a rose or a [daisy].

DEFINING RELATIONSHIP AS HIERARCHY

What I saw over and over again from people who were hurting and then I noticed it later too, is that when these people had come to define a relationship, it is *always* in the form of hierarchy. That is, somebody is up and somebody is down.

Just to give a picture to this, I would like, to have three men and three women, if you will come up here please and put your life in my hands for a moment. As I said, I've never lost anybody . . . So now, you are Cathy and you are Carlos. I'm going to make you the male/female pair. And the two men please, to be over here, and the two women over on the other side.

Now are you aware that these are the only possible combinations you can have? You're either with another man or woman if you are a man. If you're a woman, you're either with a man or another woman. There just isn't anything else. And no matter if you call this a husband and wife, a brother and a sister, a boss and a worker, a teacher and a student. You call these two brothers, workers, father and son. The same over here, these could be sisters, could be mother and daughter, could be grandmother and granddaughter, it could be teacher/student, it could be boss/worker. It doesn't matter because we've only got three possibilities. That makes things easy, that you've only got three possibilities. I'd like you to be in touch with that.

Now I can also call these people names like paranoid, schizophrenic, inadequate. I could call them by colors: black, white, blue. So what is essential, however, is that these [three pairings] are all the possibilities there are, no matter what else you put into it. These three are basic.

There's one other basic thing, and I'm going to ask you to take it on faith because of something you know in yourself. Every single one of them has a navel. I've looked everywhere over the world, and I find that everyone has a navel. Now that's a piece of something, you see, I am now telling you, but I know it's based on fact. There are a few people who had their navels removed but that was after the fact.

It's very important–and I mean this very seriously–to remember that the navel is what unites us. Because the navel means that we all came the same way. We all come by the union of a man and woman and that zygote itself is always the same: It came from an egg and a sperm. And that, itself, was a comment on what I call . . . you can use the biblical term and call it "everlasting life," you can call it "eternal life," you can call it "life-force," whatever you want. It's the egg and the sperm that contains the life, nothing else, and when those two get together it acts like a . . . glue and you know what happens. Except it doesn't glue, it just yeasts.

So they've all got navels and there's only these three possibilities of where you can be, and really only two for each person. But three for the whole world. So next time you see a family, just think about them first of all in terms of male and female. Forget about their titles. The titles are what get you off. And then think about their navels. And that will help you to have a consistent, loving relationship because you'll always be connected with life force when you remember the navel. That's by the way, a good thing when you're facing a group. Remember they all have navels.

Now, people have to have a way of going [with each other]. Some of you may be acquainted with my writing on communication–I just got that from looking at people and watching them. And I found that the majority of people, in fact almost all people with a few exceptions, engage in similar ways of handling the relationship between the two people [because they have defined the relationship as hierarchy: one up and one down].

[*Virginia demonstrates by putting people in the stances to illustrate the stress ballet*][1]

DISCUSSION AFTER DEMONSTRATION

You know, I must tell you one thing. Ashley Montague wrote a book on touching . . . Ashley Montague is an anthropologist . . . in which he documents the need for people to have touch experience. And so I would recommend this. There are people who get touch all mixed up with sex. It is a part of sex but it is by no means the whole thing. And I would recommend, if you don't know it, that you read Ashley Montague's book on touching. And I also want to remind you of something Bob Hope said. Bob Hope's one of our heroes, you know. He said, "That man wasn't cuddled so he curdled." I just thought I would put that out. . . .

It would be natural if relationships were like that [based on hierarchy, one up and one down and referring back to the demonstration] for there to be fear, envy, resentment, and in serious cases, revenge or "Wait till I get on the top! Wait till I get to be 21!" You listen for these things. Also, there's got to be some feeling of inadequacy, and one of the big things is the terrible loneliness, because, [in reality,] you have no partner: [no one separate and equal]. That may not be really understood . . . But if these other feelings–feelings of fear, envy, inadequacy–are not understood as issuing from the relationships: that is [the specific styles in which the people are communicating], they will think [these negative feelings related to the power issues] are something from the outside. This is one of the things that happens. People come to me and they quarrel about money. They think money is the issue. The issue is who's got the right to tell them what to do.

Now these all involve issues of trust and hope. You can't trust anybody you fear, you can't hope for anybody who envies, you can't join anyone that you feel inferior toward. No way. So the things that we would like to have we can't possibly have when we engage in these . . . [communication styles which imply . . . that relationship is: "I'm up; you're down" or "You're up; I'm down."]

Two years, later, in 1983, Virginia gave another mini-lecture on this subject following the live demonstration by role players. She wanted to make the point that none of us have to accept what another person says about us or to us–"they are not the deciders of me."

RELATIONSHIP BETWEEN FEELINGS
OF WORTHLESSNESS AND ABUSE

[I do not have to accept what another person says about me or to me because] they are not the deciders of me. [They do not give the final shape to how we relate.]

Most of us have been brought up with the blame right from the cradle in some way or another and so it is closely associated with survival.

So if you feel the gut turn [in response to angry blaming], that still doesn't mean you are off balance . . . if you feel bad [about that turn in the gut], you are off balance. But that one [situation] where you feel like nothing and you feel your life is at stake, that is where . . . all the seeing and hearing goes [lose contact with the other–not using your own senses]. And that is when murders get committed with people, that is when the horrible acts take place. And it sounds a little bit to me like when people get that angry with each other and they can't hear each other and the survival question is so strong, that is how wars come. . . .

CONFLICT

. . . A conflict . . . is a different way of communicating. If this one is 14 or 16 years old and her mother says she needs to be home at 5 o'clock, and she would like to come back at 6:30, at this point there is a conflict occurring. [But] remember conflict does not dictate the way of communicating because you can handle conflict in all these other ways, [that is, as demonstrated in the stress ballet demonstration].

Conflict does not dictate how you handle the communication because you can handle conflict in very flowing, congruent ways. But these two [role players], starting where they started, [will probably be unable to deal with conflict without putting blame into it]. Just try to keep that in your mind, *conflict and blaming are not equal.* Blaming is only one way to handle a conflict, usually not the best way. . . .

. . . What I am giving you here is a laboratory on how we can begin to respond to what is out there. And since blaming is the most frequent thing used . . . and I can show you . . . different ways of blaming. It doesn't matter it is all the same thing, because all . . . carries threat with it, if you are open to threat. And we are all fresh enough from our own childhood . . . to be vulnerable at least to the feeling, if not to the [lack of a sense of] self-worth.

[Spoken to two role players]: So over here is the blaming response. You, at this point, for your own health and life . . ., need to find a way to get to her without reducing yourself and hopefully, enhancing her. But at this moment it is really a struggle for you, isn't it, to be able to be straight about that? *And also there is a fine line in this straightness, not to feel that you are chicken.* Now that is an English expression that means if somebody is going to attack you, you are going to attack them back. You don't run away from a fight! You stay there and fight, this kind of thing. So many people mix up *the centered position with the placating position.* I know when I used to work with young gangs, that was always one of the things that I would help them know. Sometimes we think we are being straight when we actually are not. . . .

BEING STRAIGHT [CONGRUENT]

But you here in this position of a therapist who was straight–or a parent or somebody who was in the guiding position. [Gives example of therapist claiming congruence but is not behaving congruently.] That is typical of therapists. You know when you are in trouble with your patients, that is mostly the reason why [therapist's incongruence is not in awareness]. So that means we will spend a lot of time to be able to really get in touch with what that means.

The person who is centered has the responsibility because they have the knowledge and they have the awareness to be able to be the one to change what goes on. That is what the therapist does because you have more to bring to [the situation]. The other person can't change because they can't see and hear very well, yet they are doing the best they can (1983, p. 171).

NOTE

1. This is the term Virginia used to describe the motions through which a given dyad would go, shifting among the four incongruent communication styles in response to stress. A person might start out with placation and, rise to her/his feet, so to speak, and launch into blaming, then resort to the robot-like stance of super-reasonable behavior or irrelevant behavior–then change again. Changes would often be in response to the dyad partner's given stance.

REFERENCES

Satir, V. (1981). Virginia Satir at the University of Utah. Unpublished transcript.

Satir, V., & Banmen, J. (1983). *Virginia Satir verbatim 1984.* (Transcript of the Process Community III in Crested Butte, CO). North Delta, BC, Canada: Delta Psychological Services (11213 Canyon Crescent; V4E2R6).

Vicariously Traumatized:
Male Partners of Sexual Abuse Survivors

Audrey Diane Bloom
Randall Lyle

SUMMARY. This article suggests that male partners of female sexual-abuse survivors may become vicariously traumatized in long term relationships with childhood abuse survivors. Drawing parallels to the symptomology of PTSD and the process of transmission, this article theorizes that highly conflictual home environments may be sufficient to cause distressing psychological and behavioral changes in family members. In these relationships, male partners suffer decrements in self-esteem, power, isolation, and sexual adequacy similar to other sufferers of PTSD. No empirical information is presented, but implications for counseling "dual trauma" couples is included. *[Article copies available for a fee from The Haworth Document Delivery Service: 1-800-342-9678. E-mail address: <getinfo@haworthpressinc.com> Website: <http://www.HaworthPress.com> © 2001 by The Haworth Press, Inc. All rights reserved.]*

KEYWORDS. Partners, child sexual abuse, survivors, vicarious traumatization, relationships

Audrey Diane Bloom, MEd, LPC, NCC, ACS, is a PhD student, St. Mary's University, San Antonio, TX.

Randall Lyle, PhD, is Clinical Director, Marriage and Family Therapy Program, St. Mary's University, San Antonio, TX.

Address correspondence to: St. Mary's University, Department of Counseling and Human Services, One Camino Santa Maria, San Antonio, TX 78228.

[Haworth co-indexing entry note]: "Vicariously Traumatized: Male Partners of Sexual Abuse Survivors." Bloom, Audrey Diane, and Randall Lyle. Co-published simultaneously in *Journal of Couples Therapy* (The Haworth Press, Inc.) Vol. 10, No. 1, 2001, pp. 9-28; and: *The Abuse of Men: Trauma Begets Trauma* (ed: Barbara Jo Brothers) The Haworth Press, Inc., 2001, pp. 9-28. Single or multiple copies of this article are available for a fee from The Haworth Document Delivery Service [1-800-342-9678, 9:00 a.m. - 5:00 p.m. (EST). E-mail address: getinfo@haworthpressinc.com].

VICARIOUSLY TRAUMATIZED

Since the women's movement "uncovered" the issue of sexual abuse 30 years ago, there has been a proliferation of research surrounding childhood sexual abuse and its long-term impact on survivors. It is now estimated that perhaps one in four females and one in six males are sexually abused before eighteen years of age (Mennen & Pearlmutter, 1993; Talmadge & Wallace, 1991). It has also been widely reported in the literature that anger, distrust, depression, sleep disturbances, dissociation, sexual dysfunction, self-mutilation, addictions, and relationship difficulties are common recurrent responses to childhood sexual abuse.

Because practitioners now recognize that many abuse survivors continue to suffer a myriad of psychological and physiological manifestations of abuse decades after the initial trauma, recently much research has focused on the issue of Post Traumatic Stress Disorder. While not all victims of childhood or adult sexual abuse experience ongoing psychological sequelae (Browne & Finklehor, 1986), the incidence of PTSD in individuals who have experienced sexual trauma is well documented (Barnes, 1995; Daniel, 1996). One study (Foa, Olasov, & Steketee cited in Barnes, 1995) reports that sexual assault victims constitute the largest single group of PTSD sufferers, with 60% of sexual abuse victims meeting the criteria for PTSD at some point in their lives.

Through this research, it is also becoming increasingly clear that trauma and the manifestations of trauma are more complex than previously reported. For example, it is now recognized that PTSD and trauma responses are "contagious" (Maltas & Shay, 1995) and, once traumatized a person appears to be more vulnerable to consecutive traumas (Messman & Long, 1996). Moreover, as clinicians are becoming aware of the symptomology and etiology of PTSD, it is becoming apparent that many couples who present for couples' therapy may be, in fact, "dual trauma couples." In these couples, both partners have experienced trauma or multiple traumas that continues to impact their individual and relationship functioning.

Researchers are beginning to recognize that there may be more than one type of PTSD and more than one route of transmission (Nelson & Wright, 1996). Figley's (1985) work with the families of Vietnam veterans suggests that there are four possible ways that family members might come to demonstrate symptoms quite similar to PTSD. The first type of transmission is the *simultaneous effect* of trauma in which all members of the family are affected by the same traumatic event. Catastrophes such as natural disasters, auto accidents, and fires are examples of this type of transmission. The second type of transmission, *vicarious effects,* occurs when catastrophe strikes a family member who is not in contact with the family; war and coal mine accidents are examples of this. The third way, a *chiasmal effect* or *secondary traumatization,* occurs when the traumatic stress appears to infect the entire family making contact with the victimized family member. This route of transmission is typified by the partners of Vietnam veterans and might also be the path of transmission of trauma for partners of sexual abuse survivors. The fourth trauma, *intrafamilial trauma,* occurs when catastrophe strikes from within the family. Figley maintains that abuse, incest, and domestic violence all can result in this type of traumatization. He adds that "not only are all members of the family affected, but often the most traumatized members are denied minimal social support" (p. 411).

Matakis (1988) suggests that partners may become traumatized because they are strained as they take on the role of over-worked managers of their chaotic, stressful families. As a result, the partners–like the survivors–suffer a great deal of pain, fear, anger, depression, sexual dysfunction, lack of emotional intimacy, substance abuse and domestic violence. Solomon et al. (1992) also reported that combat veterans' partners experienced symptoms similar to those associated with PTSD, including psychiatric symptoms of somatization, depression, obsessive-compulsion problems, anxiety, paranoid ideation, and hostility, as well as impaired social functioning. They found that the unique circumstances of having someone with PTSD in their family places the partners at risk for feelings of isolation, loneliness, alienation, low self-esteem, hopelessness, a great sense of guilt for their survival or their inability to ameliorate the survivor's PTSD. Overall, these partners tend to be less happy, less satisfied, and experience greater distress than partners of those without a diagnosis of PTSD. Critical themes that emerged during Nelson and Wright's (1996) treatment of partners were problems with excessive caretaking, rigid gender roles, heightened survivor skills, and psychological symptoms similar to PTSD. Interpersonal problems, coping with the survivor's

PTSD symptoms, having their own needs unmet, violent outbursts, and emotional abuse were also critical problems in these relationships.

Despite the growing recognition of the prevalence of sexual abuse, the severity of symptoms in survivors, and the fact that systems theorists have traditionally viewed abuse as affecting all members of a family system, little attention in the literature has been devoted to the unique issues of partners of sexual abuse survivors as vicarious trauma survivors. Typically in couples therapy that includes an abuse survivor, the survivor, as the identified patient, becomes the intense focus of intervention while the partner becomes primarily an ally or an adjunct therapist. Because it has been stressed in the literature that the survivor's healing is paramount, limited attention has been devoted to the partner's role in the dyadic process of recovery. In fact, Reid, Wampler, and Taylor (1996) report that in many cases, partners have been advised explicitly or implicitly to take a secondary role and to be there primarily for the survivor (Dolan, 1991, p. 41).

Since little attention has been devoted to specifically investigating the notion of vicarious traumatization of partners of sexual abuse and its subsequent contribution to conflicted relationships, this paper will focus on the unique issues of partners of sexual abuse survivors. It will explore the responses of male partners who are attempting to maintain their disintegrating relationships and salvage their damaged identity while receiving little support or recognition of their involvement in a traumatizing family system. While this paper will offer no empirical evidence to suggest that partners of sexual abuse survivors suffer from vicarious transmission of PTSD, it will present relevant theoretical support in four areas: (a) damaged self-esteem, (b) feelings of powerlessness, (c) feelings of isolation, and (d) feeling sexually flawed. In conclusion, implications for therapy will be presented.

First, however, the following case study is presented to illustrate the complexity of dyads in which one member is a survivor of childhood incest. The case of Mitchell exemplifies how self-esteem, power, isolation, and sexual identity can be problematic in these relationships.

Mitchell is an articulate 37-year-old, Anglo male who earns a comfortable income as a computer programmer for a medical supply company. His father is a psychologist and his mother was a traditional stay-at-home mother. He and Alice have been married fourteen years and have three children, a daughter, age 12, a son, age 10, and a daughter age 5.

When Mitchell presented for treatment, he stated that he used to think his wife was "the crazy one," but he now believes that he must be crazy or some kind of freak to find himself in such an inescapable situation. He stated that, although he loves his wife, he was unsure if he could continue to live with her because family life had become too chaotic for him. He said that prior to the marriage, he had known that his wife had been victimized as a child, but he thought he could help her get over it; therefore, he never dreamed that her experience could become *the* controlling factor in their lives. Now he is angry because he feels as if they are living with a "tar baby" that shows up in places one would never expect. He said that, although his wife has been in therapy for years, her therapy makes it worse for him because she comes home from therapy full of anger about all men and then dumps her anger on him.

During their marriage, they have moved several times in hopes of finding some place where Alice could feel comfortable, but the problems follow them wherever they go at what he called "an exponential rate." Now that the children are getting older, it seems that everyone in the family is out of control. He attributes this to the fact that his wife has taught the children that they don't have to blindly follow rules just because some adult with authority told them that they must. As a result, their teachers and neighbors don't like his children or his wife.

He said that, ironically, although Alice believes that she is teaching the children never to become submissive victims, she is also trying to control everyone and everything in their environment with a rule of some sort that must be followed–except for those times when it does not have to be followed. He described it as living in an "Alice in Wonderland World" where nothing was as it appeared to be. For example, among other things, there are rules about who is "safe" and who is "unsafe"; when they are "safe" and when they are "unsafe"; who the children may play with and under which conditions; which doors and windows must be shut and locked at all times; which lights must be left on all night; which person is allowed in the bathroom with another; who is permitted in which bedroom; what type of clothing and underwear they are required to wear at all times; and which type of soap and colognes they are permitted to use. And, then there were exceptions to all of them. He said that there were so many rules that he could never keep them straight; as a result, he is constantly messing up even when he is trying his best to cooperate. His wife has blamed him so many times that now he is beginning to feel like a perpetrator of sorts–especially about sex. He said that there are so many rules about sex and the cleansing, deodorizing, and touching of body parts that he has given up on sex all together for the past year. Now, he spends all his free time playing computer games and hoping that he will not be called upon to provide childcare or to settle another dispute. Because of his wife's spending habits, he can no longer afford the recreational drugs that used to provide temporary escape for him. Now, he describes himself as a prisoner without an escape plan, bereft of self-esteem and power.

DAMAGED SELF-ESTEEM

A recurrent theme in therapy with male partners of sexual abuse survivors is that they feel like failures because they have been unable to rescue their partners from the psychological distress that ends up controlling their lives. Rice and Rice (1985) report that in our culture most partners typically bring a "love will conquer all fantasy or expectation" to their marriages that ultimately sets up the couple for feelings of failure when it becomes apparent that the impossible is, indeed, impossible. This fantasy appears to be especially apparent in the relationships of trauma survivors because both survivors and partners tend to use such terms as "the Knight in Shining Armor" or "the White Knight" or "the hero" when describing their expectations about their loving relationship rescuing the survivor from the distress of childhood sexual abuse. With the expectation that simply finding the right partner and loving them will provide recovery from the pain of childhood sexual abuse, it is easy to understand why both members express such depths of disillusionment and shame when the fantasy inevitably dies (Blume, 1988; Courtois, 1988).

As a result of the failure to find the magical solution to ameliorate the myriad conflicting feelings resulting from childhood sexual abuse, many couples may, at least initially, engage in a "conspiracy of silence" to keep the experience suppressed. Unfortunately, when the partners use denial as a defense system, the abuse issues may continue to be acted out in the relationship (Nelson & Wright, 1996). These reenactments or repetition compulsions generally result in continuous chaos, yet because the family typically does not recognize this or directly address the reason for the chaos, there is no way to reduce the oscillating cycle of stress. As a result, both members become increasingly dissatisfied with their interactions and begin a process of blaming themselves or their partners, occasionally escalating to the point of violence. Nelson and Wright (1996) point out that although physical aggression is frequently a problem in PTSD families; yet, the occurrence of verbal and emotional abuse is probably greater.

Partners typically do not understand the dynamics of sexual abuse and the resultant behavioral manifestations, but they hope to find some solution to ameliorate the survivor's pain. They may make increasingly frustrated or minimizing comments and advise the survivor to engage in simplistic solutions or to just forget about the abuse so the problems "can go away" (Courtois, 1988). However, offering advice that discounts the original traumatic experience frequently exacerbates the stress because it tends to escalate the survivor's anxiety level as it begins to replicate the denial system and the secretive environment of her family of origin and takes away her power to assert herself on her own behalf. Minimizing the extent or validity of her pain may also cause her to question her reality and her feelings of competence. Generally, this exacerbates the conflict in the household because neither partner can then directly confront their feelings or the situation. As a result, both partners suffer because neither has the permission to express their feelings directly or honestly.

Barcus (1997) asserts that most male partners generally suffer silently, vaguely aware of some ill-defined malaise, yet unable or unwilling to articulate it. In complying with the cultural expectation of a real man who suffers silently in our culture, their feelings of sorrow, pain, and frustration are often denied or suppressed as they endeavor to maintain their lives. The men may also feel betrayed by the survivor because they never expected to find themselves in this situation. In other words, the male partner's response to his inability to rescue the survivor is often similar to the young incest survivor's response to the initial abuse in her family of origin: denial and feelings of betrayal by a trusted loved one.

Barcus (1997) also reports that over the years male partners become frustrated and increasingly angry because the survivor's traumatic experience often becomes the family's priority after "it consistently affected every area of their lives" (p. 318). As demonstrated in the case of Mitchell, partners report that after awhile, it spills into all facets of their lives–work, parenting, intimacy, and social activities–until just about everything in their lives seems to revolve around the emotional fall-out from the abuse. Consequently, according to Barcus, all the "normally assumed processes in couples" are sabotaged by trauma in these relationships. For example, any simple act that non-traumatized couples would take for granted, such as hugging or play-fully teasing one another, may trigger flashbacks or trauma memories for one or both partners. Barcus also found that many partners re-ported that they spent a large portion of their lives constantly trying to adapt to their wives' emotional fluctuations or mood swings. He also indicated that in these relationships, communication skills, nurturance, problem solving, and conflict resolution skills may be underdeveloped or they might disappear completely under the pressure of trauma re-sponses. Hypervigilance and sleep disturbances further complicate an increasingly distressful way of life.

Balcom (1996) asserts that the most common characteristic of dual trauma couples is their intense emotional reactivity and their enact-ments of repetitive patterns. Thus, to these couples, it may begin to feel as if they are engaged in a never-ending circular argument or pattern of destructive behavior. More importantly, *every* family mem-ber in the system becomes affected by the trauma being played out in the system because volatile mood shifts, depression, withdrawal, and anger pervades everything and everyone, including the children. The process of multigenerational transmission of trauma can easily be-come a reality as the ensuing atmosphere of conflict and estrangement between the parents extracts a toll on the children. The heightened stress levels of both partners can make them impatient, short-tem-pered, and irritable in the face of the normal demands of the children. As a result, the children may, unwittingly, become objects of the displaced emotions by *both* parents.

Barcus (1997) reported that in addition to holding full-time jobs, the men in his group often found themselves compensating for the survi-vor's parenting deficits or becoming the primary parent for extended periods of time. Because the men may not have been initially well bonded to their children, and this is not a role that they were prepared to handle, their parenting skills became another source of contention between the couple. He reported that, in addition to ongoing parental dilemmas, these men also struggled with the issue of how to handle the sensitive and complex abuse issues with the children. The partners reported that they had much difficulty explaining what was wrong with the mother and why her behavior and outbursts were unpredictable. Similar concerns and possibilities arise with extended family members, especially those who live nearby (Nelson, 1994).

Another important reason that fathers sometimes have difficulty meeting the demands of parenthood is because they are self-conscious around their children. Fathers report that they begin to feel increasingly nervous anytime that the child needs assistance in the bathroom or while dressing because the survivor watches their every move. Because women who were sexually abused as children often develop distorted views about themselves and others, and they have difficulty trusting men–including their partners–anyone who interacts with her children may come under intense scrutiny.

Ingram (1985) describes this overall situation as a classic double bind for partners because abused women sometimes feel that they do not deserve satisfying relationships with men and cannot trust them; yet, at the same time, they overvalue men and seek them as protectors for themselves and their children. Ultimately, both members may begin to question who they are and what kind of person they are to find themselves in this situation with this person.

POWERLESSNESS

Because men are more used to seeking an active solution, the role of the supporter, who backs his wife's efforts, is often unfamiliar to men more accustomed with taking action (Barcus, 1997). Frequently, these men want to do "something" or to confront the perpetrator, yet this is often met with resistance by the survivor who wishes to handle things in her own way. Complicating this issue is the fact that these men frequently have difficulty understanding the ambivalence their partners feel toward their abusive family members. Due to the survivors' unusual relationships with their perpetrators, it is possible that the survivor expresses outrage about her abusive family member while at the same time demonstrating her unfulfilled desire for unqualified support and nurturance from her perpetrator. This double bind frequently replicates the original interactional patterns of their families of origin further, pulling the partner into the role of a hapless victim/perpetrator. The end result is confusion for both members of the dyad.

Typically, survivors come from home environments that were very insecure; thus, they develop the view that their families and the world are unsafe places. Tinling (1990) suggests that as a child, survivors were frequently preoccupied with safeguarding themselves rather than focused on learning to cooperate with others. As a result, much of her behavior is oriented toward alleviating insecurity and making her immediate world a safe place. Because this pattern is maintained in adulthood, partners of survivors may report experiences similar to that of Mitchell: that they feel controlled because there is a rule for everything–regardless of how petty it is–and all rules must be followed. Layton (1995) theorizes that victims of repeated abuse need rules because victims tend to split the world into victims, abusers, and rescuers, who are locked in a dialectical dance. She enacts and reenacts relational patterns whereby she is sometimes the victim, sometimes the abuser, and sometimes the rescuer.

Women who were sexually abused tend to be preoccupied with issues of power; thus, power struggles may become common place in these relationships. Frequently these women exhibit a heightened desire or need for power as well as a need to see themselves as capable of exerting power, yet, at the same time, they are conflicted because they are frightened by that power. Power becomes an organizing theme of the relationships that they enter into, and the need for and the fear of power is central to how they engage in and provoke particular kinds of interactions. For those males who adhere to a patriarchal power structure in the family or those males who may have difficulty relinquishing power, the potential for domestic violence is great.

As in the case of Mitchell, partners also report that even in relationships without violence, they sometimes feel like a perpetrator because they get blamed for so many things. This is because, without realizing it, survivors may often target their intimate partner to receive the anger and resentments they have about the abuse and the offender (Maltz, 1991). In fact, Maltz maintains that to some degree most survivors tend to confuse the partners with the offender because the partner presents an available and relatively safe person to release those feelings on to. Frequently, the partners have borne the brunt of the survivor's displaced or projected anger so much that they begin to feel that they deserve it.

Both the survivor and the partner may begin to feel that they are traumatically bound to one another as in a version of a "Hostage Syndrome" in which both feel that they have been taken hostage and then develop an emotional bond and a sense of allegiance with their captors. Worse yet, if the survivor is also suicidal, this may exacerbate the belief that an unfair warden is holding them prisoner. If the survivor engages in self-mutilation or self-destructive behavior, partners may feel that they are being held hostage by an out of control or crazy person. If the survivor dissociates and sometimes believes that the partner *is* the perpetrator, then the partner may begin to question his own power and sanity. Just as the survivor may inappropriately blame herself for the childhood sexual abuse, the partner may inappropriately begin to blame himself for his inability to rescue both of them.

ISOLATION

Trauma survivors often experience a profound sense of alienation from other people and the world in general (McCann & Pearlman, 1990). In the case of survivors, this is because they frequently identify themselves as being different or somehow abnormal, and accordingly, they develop ways of relating to people that does not invite companionship. They may not have learned age-appropriate skills or effective and assertive means of communicating. They may have difficulty with intimacy. Since they struggle to create boundaries or generate the courage to set appropriate limits, they find it difficult to discover cooperative solutions to life's problems (Silon, 1992). Despite all the chaos and difficulties in the relationship that could serve as incentives to seek comfort or guidance outside the relationship, male partners often become increasingly isolated because they are too embarrassed to seek existing support by talking about their spouse's behaviors to family or friends. Barcus (1997) found that they are especially prone to keeping secret the way those behaviors had eroded the level of intimacy in the relationship.

Balcom (1996) suggests that one way in which trauma affects couples is by creating extreme boundaries between the couple and the outside world. Either too rigid or too fluid, the boundaries make it difficult for normal exchanges to transpire within the couple or between the couple and outsiders. In other words, it becomes an internal situation of her against him, but them (the couple) against the external world. He also suggests that when rigid boundaries prohibit the normal expression of feelings, there is the potential to retraumatize both members who may have become more vulnerable to feelings of abandonment through their isolation and reliance on only one another for support.

Talmadge and Wallace (1991) theorize that, as an adult, the survivor may be out of touch with her internal frame of reference; consequently, she may look to her partner to define who she is and what is happening between the two of them. This neediness, coupled with isolationist behaviors, may feel overwhelming to the partner and result in additional isolationist tactics on his part. In order to protect himself, he may become over involved in his work or in a recreational activity that takes him away from the home.

DISSATISFYING SEXUAL RELATIONSHIPS

Dissatisfying sexual relationships is the last and probably most problematic area for sexual abuse survivors and their partners to be considered here. While there is continuing discussion about this point, Courtois (1988) has reported that 80% of the victims of childhood sexual abuse experienced some difficulty in adult sexual relationships. Other estimates by Becker, Skinner and Able (cited in Sarwer & Durlak, 1996) place the range at about 50% of female survivors. Difficulties range from hypoarousal, to aversion of genitals and painful sex, to orgasm disorders, and dissociation during sex. Kinzl, Traweger and Biebl (1995) found that women who experienced recurrent sexual abuse often reported intimacy disturbances (i.e., impairment by shame and a sense of guilt, disgust, anxiety), and impairment of sexual pleasure. Nevertheless, despite a negative attitude toward men and sexuality, they report that many childhood sexual abuse survivors often maintained a sexual relationship without enjoying it. Buttenheim and Levendosky (1994) confirm Mitchell's experience when they describe the sexless marriage as another manifestation of the survivor's difficulties with sexuality.

Talmadge and Wallace (1991) point out that the most basic needs of trust, openness, intimacy, reciprocity, and closeness are met or frustrated in the sexual union. Because of the abuse and its concomitant violation of body boundaries, the survivor feels alienated from her physical self, and her body becomes an object for the use of others. She does not feel desired by sexual interest in her, but rather threatened, used, and objectified.

Buttenheim and Levendosky (1994) suggest that because survivors' trust was betrayed by loved ones in their family of origin, it is often difficult for survivors to feel trusting toward the partners they choose. Because their bodies and, particularly, their sexual selves were the route by which their betrayal took place, survivors are ambivalent about sexual feelings (their own and their partner's) and view sexual activity not as a means of coming together with a cherished other, but as an opportunity for coercion, exploitation, and shame.

Talmadge and Wallace (1991) report that emotional blunting, loss of emotional and physical feeling, psychological and physical pain, distrust of others' intentions, poor self-concept, fears and phobias associated with sex, and generalized fear responses including terror and dissociation are common post-trauma responses for sexual assault victims. They further indicate that flashbacks, intrusive thoughts, and dissociation may mar survivors' current sexual relationships. For the couple, having the survivor triggered while engaging in sex can become a horrifying experience that begins a cycle of anticipatory fear and rejection.

On the other extreme, some survivors may be overly preoccupied with sex and act out sexually by engaging in self-destructive behavior (Mennen & Pearlmutter, 1993). Those members who were raised in homes where sexual boundaries were fluid may act inappropriately or dress inappropriately in front of their children. Some survivors learned at a young age to associate sex with alcohol and violence; consequently, they may display a pattern of drinking, becoming violent and engaging in wild sex with harmful partners (Kasl, 1990). Other survivors can enjoy sex only if they are in charge. Still others report that sex is only enjoyable with a partner with whom they are *not* emotionally intimate because it is only through anonymous sex that she can avoid emotional vulnerability. For these partners, the survivor's sexual addictions or infidelities are emotionally exhausting and may wear down the partner's efforts to keep the relationship going.

For male partners, the sexual problems can become overwhelming because they may begin to doubt their own sexual attractiveness and adequacy. According to Maltz (1988), even when they know intellectually that the survivor's sexual issues relate primarily to the past, many partners have to constantly battle inner tendencies to feel that they themselves are personally being sexually rejected or responsible for the trauma. As a result, they may begin to question their self-worth and wonder if they can be accepted and loved for who they are. Maltz adds that partners often feel insulted that on some level they are perceived as an offender. They also may feel that their identity and good intentions have been discounted. They begin to question whether their own needs are weird or perverted, and they become ashamed for wanting or needing sex at all. In fact, in a sort of role reversal, some partners report that they feel that they have been reduced to an object or just a penis, and they are merely seen as wanting sex and willing to do anything for it. Consequently, they may become angry or sad when they realize that the survivor believes their desire for physical contact is simply a desire for sex. Moreover, they feel tremendous guilt if they trigger the survivor or do something that may cause her to dissociate. In an attempt to prevent emotional or sexual distress, they may decide that it is easier to avoid sex, the survivor, and the relationship.

COUNSELING IMPLICATIONS

Because of the possibility of retraumatization, counseling sexual abuse survivors and trauma survivors is very sensitive taxing work, the following recommendations are made. The first is that therapists need to be fully cognizant of the etiology and manifestations of *both* sexual abuse and PTSD in order to recognize dual-trauma couples when they present for treatment. Because of the reciprocal nature of the trauma and the possibility of retraumatization, it is essential that it be recognized from the first session that both members of the couple have psychological and behavioral problems worthy of recognition and therapeutic intervention. Equally important, neither member should be considered the primary client with the most disturbing pain; nor should either member be labeled responsible or blamed for initiating the problem. The experience of neither partner should be minimized or subsumed for the greater good of the other. These couples present unique challenges for practitioners because when one partner is stable, the other may be in crisis. Or, equally plausible, one partner may progress rapidly while the other remains captive to the trauma.

The first task of the therapist should be containment of the highly emotional reactive process that has probably been spinning out of control. Exploring feelings and seeking resolution of old hurts at this time would intensify that process; thus, the first tasks should be solutions to concrete household problems. While both partners should be validated immediately for the extreme measures that they have resorted to in order to save their relationship, it is during later sessions that both members could more readily benefit from learning how they perpetuate their part in the recursive drama in which they are engaged.

It is important to note that when partners were asked to provide suggestions for future therapeutic interventions with other partners in the same situations, partners recommended that the first task of any therapeutic intervention be educational (Reid, Wampler, & Taylor, 1996). They requested fundamental education about sexual abuse in order to understand the ramifications of childhood sexual abuse on both survivors and partners, plus information on the likely course of therapy. Education, in this case, provides containment and a forum for understanding previously inexplicable behavior and feelings. It normalizes their experience and may reduce self-blame and isolation. This new framework may also provide the basis for empowerment, which may permit optimism to resurface. Completion of genograms devoted to sexual issues of both partners and their families is an excellent tool to begin this process.

The other essential primary task is for both members to become cognizant of the harm their emotional drama is causing their children, and both should be reminded to establish the children's welfare as the priority in their future interactions. Because of the magnitude of conflict and emotional reactivity in dual trauma families, the parents should be encouraged to provide systemic solutions. This means providing a therapeutic experience for the children as well. Whether this would mean inclusion of the children into family sessions or providing separate sessions for the children would depend on the severity of the presenting issues and the ages of the children. Disclosure of the mother's past trauma and any related present difficulties should be made according to the child's age, level of maturity, level of comprehension, and available support system. Courtois (1988) warns that disclosure to children should be made only after careful consideration of motives and consequences. A risk assessment should be a therapeutic priority because if the safety of the children is at stake, they will need to be given enough information to protect themselves from any abusive family members or perpetrators.

It is essential that, at least initially, both members of the dyad have their own therapists or groups. Because both survivors and partners have begun to take on a negative couple identity, it is important that they have an opportunity to explore and reject this identity in the supportive presence of others. Groups composed of female sexual abuse survivors and groups of male partners provide excellent forums for awareness, education, and social interaction among others who have shared the same experience. Group membership also provides a normalizing experience and a place of solace and support for those times when the other member of the dyad is in crisis or at a different stage of recovery. Supportive cohorts are also important because the couple has probably become a re-traumatizing system for one another in their closed family system. Worse yet, as noted in the case of Mitchell, if only one member of the dyad participates in therapy, the negative emotions of therapy can be brought home and reinitiate the cycle of traumatization that the couple has developed. Mentors, both professional and social, should be encouraged as life long supports.

After self-esteem has improved and a support system has developed, the couple should be encouraged to engage in conjoint sessions to work on those issues unique to that couple. Because mistrust, splitting, and high emotional reactivity may still exist, working with a male-female co-therapist team with the couple may serve to reduce some of the anxiety and promote problem-solving attempts. Much attention needs to be devoted to identity changes and role changes that have occurred in the process. Both members need to shift from their victim roles and be encouraged to develop more functional behavioral patterns. Reenactment patterns need to be broken and empowering patterns substituted. Partners should be treated as equals in any learning experience, rather than one partner being permitted to patronize or parent the other.

Although it may seem somewhat simplistic, therapists should also be reminded that these couples may need to be taught fundamental concepts such as how to have fun and how to recognize fun. Because parts of the survivor's childhood were stolen from her, or she may have grown up focused primarily on the abuse experience, it is possible that she has never learned *how* to enjoy herself; thus, it is possible that they, as a couple, have never been able to be playful and experience the joy in their relationship.

A final note of caution for therapists working with highly traumatized couples. As noted by McCann and Pearlman (1990), recurrent exposure to traumatic situations through the client's memories may evoke concern about the therapist's own sense of power of efficacy in the world. And helpers with a high need for power are likely to be greatly impacted by the powerlessness reported by their clients. As a result, therapists may be inclined to inappropriately urge clients to take action rather than to understand the meanings of their responses.

Therapists working with traumatized persons should be cognizant of the process of vicarious traumatization and alert for symptoms in themselves. There is a growing body of evidence to suggest that therapists are at risk for traumatization by their clients (McCann & Pearlman, 1990). All therapists, including private practitioners, would benefit from having a clinical supervisor and a professional support system composed of other professionals who are familiar with working with trauma survivors. These counselors can provide opportunities for emotional support in addition to the professional and intellectual support they offer.

CONCLUSION

Regardless of the origin of the trauma, therapists face unique challenges in the treatment of couples in which one or both are survivors of sexual abuse. It is readily apparent that the issues involved in counseling sexual abuse survivors and their partners are complex and interrelated. It also appears that the process of secondary victimization or vicarious traumatization may be an explanation for the escalating psychological and behavioral patterns that these couples experience in long-term relationships. However, additional research is warranted before firm conclusions can be drawn. Couples therapists are in an ideal situation to provide information and understanding in this process. They can begin by acknowledging that both partners in the dyad have legitimate issues and needs.

Given the magnitude of the problems that partners face and the paucity of research on the topic, there is certainly an immediate need for professionals to gain a better understanding of this increasingly pervasive problem. As Figley (1995) pointed out, the majority of research on stress disorders has used a narrow definition of the victim; therefore, it has focused on only individuals who have most immediately experienced extreme stressors. Even though empirical research has not found conclusive evidence for PTSD in partners of PTSD sufferers, it is important to assess the characteristics, predisposing factors, and problems faced by partners of sexual abuse survivors. Because many of these families exist in extreme distress, it is essential that family therapists become fully cognizant of the ramifications of traumatizing family systems and recognize that, in addition to the survivor, sexual abuse may traumatically affect everyone and everything in their subsequent family systems.

REFERENCES

Balcom, D. (1996). The interpersonal dynamics and treatment of dual trauma couples. *Journal of Marital and Family Therapy, 22* (4), 431-442.

Balcom, D., Lee, R. G., & Tager, J. (1995). The systemic treatment of shame in couples. *Journal of Marital and Family Therapy, 21* (1), 55-65.

Barcus, R. (1997). Partners of survivors of abuse: A men's therapy group. *Psychotherapy, 34* (3), 316-323.

Barnes, M. F. (1995). Sex therapy in the couples context: Therapy issues of victims of sexual trauma. *The American Journal of Family Therapy, 23* (4), 351-360.

Blume, E. S. (1989). *Secret survivors: Uncovering incest and its aftereffects in women.* New York: Ballantine Books.

Browne, A., & Finkelhor, D. (1986). Impact of childhood sexual abuse: A review of the research. *Psychological Bulletin, 99* (1), 66-67.

Buttenheim, M., & Levendosky, A. (1994). Couples treatment for incest survivors. *Psychotherapy, 31* (3).

Cohen, T. (1995). Motherhood among incest survivors. *Child Abuse & Neglect, 19* (12), 1423-1429.

Courtois, C. A. (1997). Healing the incest wound: A treatment update with attention to recovered memory issues. *The American Journal of Psychotherapy, 51* (4), 464-497.

Courtois, C. A. (1988). *Healing the incest wound: Adult survivors in therapy.* New York: W. W. Norton.

Daniel, L. E. (1996). Treating Post-Traumatic Stress Disorder in female adult victims of childhood incest. *Family Therapy, 23* (1), 1-9.

Dolan, Y. M. (1991). *Resolving sexual abuse: Solution-focused therapy and Ericksonian hypnosis for adult survivors.* New York: W. W. Norton.

Feinauer, L. L., Mitchell, J., Harper, J. M., & Dane, S. (1996). The impact of hardiness and severity of childhood sexual abuse on adult sexual adjustment. *The American Journal of Family Therapy, 24* (3), 206-214.

Figley, C. R. (1985). *Trauma and its wake: The study and treatment of post-traumatic stress disorder.* New York: Brunner/Mazel.

Figley, C. R. (1995). *Compassion fatigue: Coping with secondary traumatic stress disorder in those who treat the traumatized.* New York: Brunner/Mazel.

Gelinas, D. J. (1983). The persisting negative effects of incest. *Psychiatry, 16,* 312-322.

Ingram, T. L. (1985). Sexual abuse in the family of origin and unresolved issues: A Gestalt systems treatment approach for couples. *Family Therapy, 12* (2), 175-183.

Kasl, C. D. (1990). *Women, sex, and addiction.* New York: Harper & Row.

Kinzl, J. F., Twageger, C., & Biebl, W. (1995). Sexual dysfunctions: Relationship to childhood sexual abuse and early family experiences in a nonclinical sample. *Child Abuse & Neglect, 19* (7), 785-792.

Layton, L. (1995). Trauma, gender, identity, and sexuality: Discourses on fragmentation. *American Imago, 52* (1), 107-125.

Maltas, C., & Shay, J. (1995). Trauma contagion in partners of survivors of childhood sexual abuse. *American Journal of Orthopsychiatry, 65* (4), 529-539.

Maltz, W. (1991). *The Sexual Healing Journey: A guide for survivors sexual abuse.* New York: Harper Collins.

Matikis, A. (1988). *Vietnam wives.* Washington, DC: Woodbine House.

McCann, I. L., & Pearlman, L. A. (1990). Vicarious traumatization: A framework for understanding the psychological effects of working with victims. *Journal of Traumatic Stress, 3* (1), 131-149.

Mennen, F. E., & Pearlmutter, L. (1993). Detecting childhood sexual abuse in couples therapy. *Families in Society: The Journal of Contemporary Human Services, 74* (2), 74-83.

Messman, T., & Long, P. (1996). Child sexual abuse and its relationship to revictimization in adult women: A review. *Clinical Psychology Review, 16* (5), 397-420.

Nadelson, C., & Polonshy, D. (1991). Childhood sexual abuse: The invisible ghost in couple therapy. *Psychiatric Annals, 21* (8), 479-484.

Nelson, J. C. (1994). One partner impaired: Implications for couple treatment. *Family Therapy, 21* (3), 185-196.

Nelson, B. S., & Wright, D. W. (1996). Understanding and treating Post-Traumatic Stress Disorder symptoms in female partners of veterans with PTSD. *Journal of Marital and Family Therapy, 22* (4), 445-476.

Reid, K. S., Wampler, R. S., & Taylor, D. K. (1996). The "alienated" partner: Responses to traditional therapies for adult sex abuse survivors. *Journal of Marital and Family Therapy, 22* (4), 443-453.

Rice, J. K., & Rice, K. G. (1986). *Living through divorce: A developmental approach to divorce therapy.* New York: Guilford Press.

Sarwer, D. B., & Durlak, J. A. (1996). Childhood sexual abuse as a predictor of adult female sexual dysfunction: A study of couples seeking sex therapy. *Child Abuse & Neglect, 20* (10), 963-972.

Silon, B. (1992). Dissociation: A symptom of incest. *Individual Psychology, 48* (2), 155-164.

Solomon, Z., Waysman, M., Levy, G., Fried, B., Mikulincer, M., Benbenishty, R.,

Florian, V., & Bleich, A. (1992). From front line to home front: A study of secondary traumatization. *Family Process, 31* (9), 289-301.

Talmadge, L. D., & Wallace, S. C. (1991). Reclaiming sexuality in female incest survivors. *Journal of Sex & Marital Therapy, 17* (3), 163-182.

Tinling, L. (1990). Perpetration of incest by significant others: Mothers who do not want to see. *Individual Psychology, 46* (1), 280-297.

The Impact of the Abuse of Males on Intimate Relationships

Aphrodite Matsakis

SUMMARY. A history of emotional and physical abuse, either in childhood or as part of a military or paramilitary experience, can profoundly affect a man's desire and capacity for intimacy and negotiation in long term relationships. Common consequences of abuse, such as observational learning of abusive behavior, identification with the aggressor, or fear of acting like the aggressor, are described in terms of their potential impact on couples. Examples are drawn from men with histories of abuse in childhood or in the military. *[Article copies available for a fee from The Haworth Document Delivery Service: 1-800-342-9678. E-mail address: <getinfo@haworthpressinc.com> Website: <http://www.HaworthPress. com> © 2001 by The Haworth Press, Inc. All rights reserved.]*

KEYWORDS. Male abuse, identification with the aggressor, abuse and relationships, child abuse, childhood sexual abuse, military training, wife abuse

INTRODUCTION

How might a history of abuse impact on a man's relationship with his wife or partner? Under these circumstances, the normal stresses of

---

Aphrodite Matsakis, PhD, has twenty-five years of counseling experience with adult survivors of child abuse, abused wives, and combat veterans. She is the author of two texts for therapists, including *Managing Client Anger* and *PTSD: A Complete Treatment Guide* and seven other books on topics such as trauma, depression, domestic violence, eating disorders and addiction, including *Survivor Guilt*, and *I Can't Get Over It: A Handbook for Trauma Survivors.*

[Haworth co-indexing entry note]: "The Impact of the Abuse of Males on Intimate Relationships." Matsakis, Aphrodite. Co-published simultaneously in *Journal of Couples Therapy* (The Haworth Press, Inc.) Vol. 10, No. 1, 2001, pp. 29-39; and: *The Abuse of Men: Trauma Begets Trauma* (ed: Barbara Jo Brothers) The Haworth Press, Inc., 2001, pp. 29-39. Single or multiple copies of this article are available for a fee from The Haworth Document Delivery Service [1-800-342-9678, 9:00 a.m. - 5:00 p.m. (EST). E-mail address: getinfo@haworthpressinc.com].

intimacy are exacerbated by the presence of ghosts. The ghosts are invisible, but they have a very real impact on the psychological well being of each member of the couple, as well as on their relationship. These "ghosts," of course, are the lingering impacts of the trauma. This article explores the ways in which being an abuse survivor creates conflict yet sometimes helps bind the couple together, as well as other special dynamics, such as identification with the aggressor.

CLINICAL BASES

This article is based on twenty-four years of private clinical work with adult male survivors of childhood abuse and individual and couples counseling with combat veterans at a Department of Veterans Affairs Medical Center and Readjustment Counseling Center. About half of the veteran sample reported a history of significant child abuse.

THE ABUSE OF MEN IN CHILDHOOD

Child abuse involves physical, emotional, and sexual abuse as well as neglect (Brunner, 1999; Children's Bureau, 1998). Although child abuse is difficult to measure, conservative estimates are that 44 per 1,000 children younger than 18 are abused annually (Children's Bureau, 1998; Brunner, 1999). However, like all forms of domestic violence, child abuse tends to be underreported. Some professionals hesitate to report suspected abuse because they fear legal entanglements or believe interventions by child protective services are likely to be ineffective and ultimately create even more hardship for a child.

Children themselves may not report the crime because they are too young; fear police and hospitals; or fear being blamed, beaten or otherwise punished for "telling." Some may have almost totally repressed their memory of abuse. Such amnesia can be physiological as well as psychological. Psychologically, the child needs to forget the abuse in order to cope with the experience and maintains some attachment to his caregiver who, although abusive, may be the child's only source of nurturance and protection. Physiologically, certain biochemical changes can occur as the result of repeated or severe trauma which induce various degrees of amnesia (Van der Kolk, Mc Farlane & Weiseath, 1996).

Why Males Tend Not to Report Abuse

Males especially tend to remain silent or be ambivalent about disclosing abuse because they do not want to be seen as powerless or suffer the shame of appearing to be passive victims. In our society, victims are not perceived as being "masculine" and the macho code of ethics require that men "take it," that is, suffer pain without complaint. Furthermore, in some families, physical and emotional abuse is an expected part of growing up male.

Finkelhor (1988) gives two additional reasons why boys tend not to report abuse: "Boys grow up with the male ethic of self reliance" and with messages such as "don't complain" or "don't have others fight your battles" (Finkelhor, 1988, p. 14). Consequently it is harder for them to seek help when they hurt. Also boys might have more to lose from telling others about being victimized, such as a decrease in social status and power.

In this sample, many men considered their childhood abuse as "normal" and became angered at any suggestion that being battered might be harmful. Sam, now forty-two, wasn't sure how often he was physically and sexually abused by his brother. He remembered a particularly violent incident in which his brother threatened to put a wire hanger in Sam's anus. According to Sam, this one-time occurrence did not mean he was an abused child and he trivialized beatings from which he emerged with bruises and broken bones as instances of "boys play." Whether or not Sam considered himself to be abused, he most definitely was. Perhaps Sam's attitude is a form of defense or denial of the impact of abuse or perhaps it is an attempt to retain an image of his abusive brother as a good person.

The Abuse of Males:
Adult Military and Paramilitary Experiences

The abuse of men extends beyond child abuse. Adult men can be abused under the guise of "training" or "initiation" into certain organizations, such as fraternities, sports teams or military and paramilitary organizations. For example, at Columbine High School in Littleton, Colorado, the site of a 1999 shoot-out which resulted in over a dozen deaths, sports initial rituals involved senior wrestlers being permitted to twist the nipples of new wrestlers until they turned purple and older tennis players being permitted to send hard volleys to younger player's backsides (Adams and Russakoff, 1999).

Abuse can also occur in boot camp and other forms of military training where physical and emotional hardships are used not only to help soldiers acquire necessary military skills, but to foster a group identity; inculcate an attitude of complete unquestioning acceptance of authority; and strengthen the body through exacting fitness programs and physical deprivation. A "real man" is expected to endure physical or emotional suffering without complaint.

According to the sampled men, however, military training and subsequent military experiences also included ridicule, beatings and other forms of assault which clearly violated military codes and which they felt bore little or no relationship to military objectives and which seemed to be expressions of an individual officer's or fellow soldier's lust for power. While they firmly believed that certain degrees of physical and emotional duress were necessary to "toughen-up" for battle, they were critical of instances where they felt that they or other soldiers were abused in a lawless or purposeless manner. Not only soldiers who were victimized, but those who observed the abuse (and felt powerless or too afraid to stop it), reported that the abuse did not build their emotional or physical fortitude, but rather demoralized and traumatized them.

Abuses incurred in military training have sometimes been defended as necessary rites of passage which have been normative in traditional and ancient societies. Like men in military training, initiates in ancient rites were removed from familiar physical surroundings and previous emotional attachments; held in captivity; and subjected to terrorist tactics, physical pain, and exposure to the elements (Campbell, 1988). However, traditional rites lasted only a few days (not weeks, months or years as does the military experience); were highly ritualized and controlled; and were usually conducted by kinsmen and neighbors, not by relative strangers. All of these factors probably mitigated the instances of individual sadism or purposeless malice (Campbell, 1988).

In ancient rites, physical force and pain were used to construct a "new identity" or a "new man," for example, an adult man from a boy, a warrior from a non-combatant identity. In contrast, as described by some of the sampled survivors, the intent of some actions in the military seemed to be to diminish, if not destroy an individual's integrity, and to severely harm his body. [Some ancient rituals did involve torture or even the death of some initiates. But even here, such acts were generally prescribed by tradition not individual caprice (Campbell, 1988).]

There are no data on the extent of such abuse in the military, real or perceived. Clearly not all soldiers or veterans counseled by this author have reported such abuse. In fact, in psychotherapy groups, discussions about having been abused during boot camp or afterwards have often shocked or surprised some group members who stated that they never experienced or witnessed lawless violence against fellow soldiers during military training. Furthermore, the observations made in this article cannot be widely generalized since they are not based on a random sample, but on help-seeking veterans who served in the 1960's and 1970's. Since 1980, the military has attempted several internal reforms in the military. Also, certain unofficial abusive practices may have been mitigated by the increased presence of women in the military, as well as by public pressure following media coverage of the deaths and maiming of soldiers during training.

MALE ABUSE AND DOMESTIC VIOLENCE

Current estimates are that anywhere from one-tenth to one-third of all married couples engage in spousal assault. However, many researchers, as well as official military and other government documents, note that wife abuse, like child abuse, tends to be underreported (Walker, 1979; Matsakis, 1996).

Men from all social groups batter–rich men, poor men, white men, African-American men, professors, and even clergymen. To date, we do not know whether veterans, whether they were abused in the military or not, batter their wives more or less than any other group of men. Yet available data indicate that wife abuse exists in the military and among veterans, as it does in the general population (Matsakis, 1996).

Abused men do not automatically become abusive themselves. According to available data, the majority of men who report being abused are not abusive to others as adults (Baron, 1999; Myers, 1999). However, being or witnessing abuse as a child or as part of military experience exposes men to the roles of victim and victimizer thus making them capable of reenacting either one or both of these roles in intimate relationships with wives or partners.

Current estimates are that approximately 30% of those abused as children go on to abuse their wives or children, a rate four times higher than the national rate of domestic violence (Kaufman and Zigler, 1987; Widom, 1989a). There are no comparable data for the military. However animal research has shown that when normally placid hamsters are repeatedly threatened and attacked while young, effects linger into adult lives. They grow up to be cowards when caged with same-size hamsters or bullies when caged with weaker ones (Myers, 1999). Such animals show changes in brain chemicals such as serotonin which calm aggressive impulses. Abused children who become aggressive teens and adults have been found to have similarly sluggish serotonin responses (Myers, 1999; Van der Kolk et al., 1996). This correlation is the result of social learning factors, such as the imitation or observational learning, and other factors, such as, identification with the aggressor and the association of emotionality with the female sex.

Identification with the Aggressor

As Walker (1979) points out, children growing up in violent homes frequently have ambivalent feelings towards the victim, whether the victim be their mother, father, siblings, another relative, or themselves. On the one hand, they may empathize with the victim's pain and wish to be protective. On the other hand, they may be repelled by the victim's helplessness. In our society where power tends to be defined as domination, children, especially male children, may come to respect and value the abuser more than the victim because of the abuser's obvious upper hand. In the military, soldiers may empathize with a new recruit who is being victimized. However, they may also admire and wish to emulate the powerful victimizer.

In homes where the father abuses both his wife and children, the children may reject and despise their mother because she is too weak to protect them. Intellectually they may realize that their mother is no match for their larger, more aggressive father. However, emotionally, they may feel their mother has betrayed them. They may then conclude that if mother cannot protect them from father, she cannot possibly protect them from other dangers either. Therefore, they may look to their father as their protector and ally with him, even if he is currently mistreating them.

Similarly, a soldier who is abused because he is fairly (or unfairly) deemed weak or unskilled might be viewed as an undesirable comrade in arms. "If I had to go into the field, I'd rather go with an SOB than some sensitive guy who couldn't take the heat," one veteran states, summing up the attitude held by many in this sample.

Identification with the aggressor also occurs because it helps fight the intolerable feelings of helplessness involved in trauma. These feelings of helplessness can provoke so much anxiety that victims can come to admire and respect the abuser. In some cases, the victim's regard for the abuser may become even greater than any empathy they have for themselves, or other victims.

The revulsion against feeling powerless is especially strong for males, for whom passivity and powerlessness are usually cultural anathemas. Also contributing to identification with aggressor is the fact that in abusive environments, non-violent means of resolving interpersonal differences and coping with other life problems are rarely modeled or otherwise taught. Usually the parents themselves do not know how to manage difficulties non-destructively. In violent homes, even when parent(s) are familiar with non-violent means of solving problems, typically there is too much turmoil in the home to permit adequate instruction of children. Furthermore, children tend to do as parents do, not as they say. The military emphasizes obeying orders, not negotiating with superiors, and offers a plentitude of violent role models.

Identification with the aggressor can also result from the child's wish for a loving nurturing parent. The abusive parent is split into two parts: the good and the bad. The child identifies with the "bad" part of the parent, leaving the illusion of having "good" parent intact (Matsakis, 1991). In the military, the soldier may see himself as "inadequate" or "unfit," thus leaving the vision of a military devoted only to patriotic and idealistic goals intact.

Emotions and Women

Another etiological factor implicated in domestic violence is the association of emotions with women. Both men abused as children or as adults, state that showing any emotion (other than anger) while being abused usually earned them the title of "fag," "sissy," "girl," "wimp," "skirt," or some other name associated with the female sex. The attitude that having emotions, expressing them, or taking them seriously, is a sign of physical, moral, and emotional weakness (alleg-edly typical of women) runs rampant in the military and paramilitary organizations, such as the police force.

Police officers who seek help are often punished, even though this goes against official policy (Kates, 1999). Similarly according to the hundreds of veterans counseled during the past twenty-five years, admitting to psychological distress and, even worse, seeking help, could mean rebuke and humiliation from peers and superiors. Combat soldiers or police officers who dared admit to strong feelings, even grief over the death of comrades, might be considered "unfit for duty" or a liability to others. They could be avoided, if not disparaged, by others. (Female soldiers and police officers also adhere to this norm of emotional stoicism in order to gain acceptance and prove their "strength.")

The devaluation of emotions and their association with femininity can trigger wife abuse when a man's feelings about having been abused (or any other emotionally powerful experience) begin to surface. At this point, he may begin to panic. Feeling out of control and emasculated (by his own emotions, which, except for his anger, he might view as "feminine") he may attempt to gain a sense of control and affirm his masculinity by battering. Battering also helps to release the mounting adrenaline caused by his pent-up emotions and inner turmoil.

"When he beats me, he's beating the woman in himself, that is the feeling part of himself, which he hates and thinks is a sign of inferiori-ty," one wife explains. "If I am upset or sad, he gets angry with me and hits me. It's like he can't stand me being emotional because he can't stand himself being emotional. The worst beating I got was the day my grandmother died and I started crying."

In Jungian terms, in assaulting his female partner, a man is attempt-ing to disown, punish, or eliminate his anima or feeling self, which he considers dangerous because it implies inferiority and, at least the past, threatened his vocational status. He may also be trying to cause pain comparable to the pain he is feeling.

Some men may try to feel strong and "manly" by attempting to control their partners by other means, such as making excessive de-mands on the woman's time, restricting her financially, or isolating her from others. However, if she resists his attempts to control her or otherwise frustrates him, he may resort to violence in order to assume a position of dominance.

ABUSE HISTORY:
ADDITIONAL IMPACT ON COUPLES

The male who has come to identify with the aggressor may turn his adult home environment into a replica of his original abuse environment. For example, some of the wives of veterans complain that their husbands treat their home as if it was boot camp, and their children, like new recruits. "He thinks he's instilling values when he yells or hits them when they make a mistake. That's how they treated him in the military, he says. But when I tell him our home isn't the military, he goes off on me and breaks things," one wife explains. Like some of the other wives, this wife complained that her husband expected complete obedience "as if he was a general or something."

Relationship problems can also arise when the wife's requests are perceived as "commands" or "orders." Suppressed hostility towards commanding officers stimulated by the wife's request may subsequently be directed towards her. This is especially the case if the wife's request is accompanied by complaints about her husband's prior performance in completing some task. On the other hand, some of the veterans developed such an aversion to criticizing or regulating others that they have great difficulty setting boundaries or disciplining children.

Wives of these men complain that their husbands leave the difficult task of child discipline entirely in their hands: "He saw so much abuse in the military and took so much too, that he lets the kids go wild. He can't bring himself to put restrictions on them or point out to them when they are wrong because it reminds him too much of what he went through. But that leaves me with the burden, which causes lots of arguments. If I raise my voice or give a little slap, he calls me 'abusive.' The kids hear him say these things, which makes discipline much harder and our marriage, much weaker."

Low Self-Esteem, Feelings of Worthlessness,
Depression and Passivity

If, instead of identifying with the aggressor, a man identifies with the victim (and continues in a victim role even when in a non-abusive situation), he is vulnerable to clinical depression and feelings of low self-worth (Kendall-Tacket, Williams & Finkelhor, 1993). Given his low self-esteem, he may feel he doesn't deserve to be cared for and may avoid relationships altogether. Or he may avoid relationships because he fears being dominated by his partner due to his own inability to say "no," or otherwise being assertive.

If a man confuses being asking for his needs to be met or otherwise being assertive with being aggressive and is loathe to act in any manner which may be deemed as "aggressive," he may be easily exploited. He may allow employers, partners, and even his children to emotionally abuse or financially exploit him. Having acquired a sense of worthlessness due to being abused, especially if abused as a child, he may not feel entitled to love, respect and fairness in his relationship and may accept mistreatment from his wife or partner without much protest. In comparison to the abuse he endured in the past, his marital unhappiness may seem "minor" and therefore, quite tolerable.

The pattern of victimization may extend to employers and friends. In cases observed, men with histories of abuse have failed to collect what is owed them from employers or debtors, have permitted former wives or girlfriends to rob them of vehicles, large sums of money or other belongings. They also tolerate verbal abuse from attorneys, physicians, mental health professionals, and members of their extended family and neighbors, as well as intimate partners. Yet they cannot easily consider leaving an emotionally abusive or financially exploitative partner or professional for fear that they are too unworthy and unlovable to find a replacement.

In some cases, frustrations about not being able to express oneself or at being mistreated accumulate to an intolerable level and erupt in the form of verbal or physical outbursts against loved ones, or even professionals. Such lack-of-control serves to confirm the man's view of himself as unworthy and unlovable, which plants the seeds for further victimization, depression, and subsequent outbreaks of abuse or violence, towards the self, or others.

REFERENCES

Adams, L. & Russakoff, D. (1999, June 12). Dissecting Columbine's cult of the athlete: In search for answers, community examines one source of killers' rage. *The Washington Post*. A1, A14.

Baron, R. A. (1998) *Psychology: Fourth edition,* Boston: Allyn & Bacon.

Brunner, B. (Ed.). (1999). *The time almanac.* Boston: Information Please LLC.

Campbell, J. (1988). *The power of myth.* New York: Doubleday.

Children's Bureau, U.S. Department of Health and Human Services. (1998). *Child maltreatment 1996: Reports from the states to the national child abuse and neglect data system.* Washington, DC: U.S. Government Printing Office.

Finkelhor, D. (1988). *Child sexual abuse: New theory and research.* New York: Free Press.

Kates, A. (1999). *Cop shock: Surviving post-traumatic stress disorder.* Tucson, AZ: Holbrook Street Press.

Kaufman, J. & Zigler, E. (1987). Do abused children become abusive parents? *American Journal of Orthopsychiatry 57,* 186-192.

Kempe, R. S. & Kempe, C. C. (1978). *Child abuse.* Cambridge, MA: Harvard University Press.

Kendall-Tackett, K., Williams, L. & Finkelhor, D. (1993). Impact of sexual abuse on children: A review and synthesis of recent empirical studies. *Psychological Bulletin, 113,* 164-180.

Matsakis, A. (1991). *When the bough breaks: A helping guide for parents of sexually abused children.* Oakland, CA: New Harbinger Publications.

Matsakis, A. (1996). *Vietnam wives: Facing the challenges of life with veterans suffering from post-traumatic stress.* Lutherville, MD: The Sidran Foundation.

Myers, D. G. (1999). *Exploring psychology: Fourth edition.* New York: Worth Publishers.

NCCAN (1988). *Executive summary: Study of national incidence and prevalence of child abuse and neglect.* Washington, DC: Government Printing Office.

Van der Kolk, B., Mc Farlane, A. C., & Weisaeth, L. (Eds.). (1996). *Traumatic stress: The effects of overwhelming experience on mind, body, and society.* New York: The Guilford Press.

Walker, L. (1979). *The battered woman.* New York: Harper & Row.

Widom, C. S. (1989a). Does violence beget violence? A critical examination of the literature. *Psychological Bulletin, 106,* 3-28.

Widom, C. S. (1989b). The cycle of violence. *Science, 244,* 160-166.

Abuse Committed by Women
Against Male Intimates

Tonia L. Nicholls
Donald G. Dutton

SUMMARY. A review of the rapidly expanding empirical research exploring the incidence, prevalence and characteristics of domestic violence committed by women against male intimates supports several conclusions: (1) the majority of abuse in intimate relationships involves mutual aggression; (2) women are as likely to aggress against partners as are men, and men are as likely as women to be the victims of intimate assaults; (3) women are more likely to be physically injured; and, (4) severe systematic abuse in intimate relationships is rare. *[Article copies available for a fee from The Haworth Document Delivery Service: 1-800-342-9678. E-mail address: <getinfo@haworthpressinc.com> Website: <http://www. HaworthPress.com> © 2001 by The Haworth Press, Inc. All rights reserved.]*

KEYWORDS. Abuse, domestic violence

VIOLENCE BY FEMALES

Results from the first National Family Violence Survey (NFVS; Straus, Gelles & Steinmetz, 1980), and many other studies that fol-

---

Tonia L. Nicholls is affiliated with the Mental Health, Law, & Policy Institute, Department of Psychology, Simon Fraser University.

Donald G. Dutton is affiliated with the Department of Psychology, University of British Columbia.

Address correspondence to: Donald G. Dutton, Department of Psychology, University of British Columbia, 2136 West Mall, Vancouver, BC, Canada V6T 1Z4 (E-mail: dutton@interchange.ubc.ca).

[Haworth co-indexing entry note]: "Abuse Committed by Women Against Male Intimates." Nicholls, Tonia L., and Donald G. Dutton. Co-published simultaneously in *Journal of Couples Therapy* (The Haworth Press, Inc.) Vol. 10, No. 1, 2001, pp. 41-57; and: *The Abuse of Men: Trauma Begets Trauma* (ed: Barbara Jo Brothers) The Haworth Press, Inc., 2001, pp. 41-57. Single or multiple copies of this article are available for a fee from The Haworth Document Delivery Service [1-800-342-9678, 9:00 a.m. - 5:00 p.m. (EST). E-mail address: getinfo@haworthpressinc.com].

lowed, indicate that women physically assault male partners as often as men physically assault female partners. These findings have been met with disbelief in part, because violence and crime is considered a masculine domain. Hotaling, Straus and Lincoln (1990) concluded that although the rate of crime and violence outside of the family is appreciably higher for men, there is a significant relationship between both mens' and womens' intrafamilial and extrafamilial violence. Hotaling and colleagues proposed that: (1) the pervasive prevalence of violence within the family; and, (2) the relationship between violence in the home and violence in the community evidence the necessity of investigating abuse by women against intimates.

Unfortunately, until recently there has been a perceptual blackout about battered husbands. We have few insights into the nature of violence by women toward men and even less insight into how to explain changes in the rates of violence toward men (Hampton, Gelles & Harrop, 1989). In their comprehensive review of the literature over the last two decades, Jasinski and Williams (1998) noted that attention to the prevalence of aggression by wives against their partners is an extremely contentious issue. They noted that feminist scholars are reluctant to acknowledge violent conflict tactics used by women due to a fear that recognizing violence by women will result in detracting attention and, therefore services, from the often severe victimization experienced by the minority of female victims of domestic violence (Jasinski & Williams, 1998). Given the deficits in the literature the rest of this paper will be dedicated to a discussion of violence by women against male intimates. This begins with an examination of the operational definition of domestic violence.

DEFINING DOMESTIC VIOLENCE

The most prolific domestic violence researchers have focused their examination of abusive intimate relationships on discrete physical acts of aggression (see for instance, Dutton, 1998; Straus & Gelles, 1990). Despite that fact, these same authors agree that significant damage can be experienced by a victim of verbal or psychological abuse. Dutton (1998) proposed that the narrow definition of domestic abuse typically used in the research does not accurately reflect the constellation of behaviours committed by abusive partners. Furthermore, an examination of physical violence alone does not accurately reflect the experience of the victim. In fact, Straus (in press) proposed that the ramifications of verbal abuse can be even more extreme than that experienced by the victim of a physical attack (e.g., suicide; see also Straus & Sweet, 1992; Vissing, Straus, Gelles, & Harrop, 1993). However, Dutton (1998) and Straus (in press) both argued that there are legal, sociological, and socio-political reasons indicating that an operational definition of domestic violence should be limited to physical aggression. Legally, the severity of the assault and degree of injury to the victim influences the likelihood of arrest and prosecution. Furthermore, the vast majority of society has clearly agreed that physical assaults are socially unacceptable, whereas there are many grey areas with regard to emotional and psychological abuse. Finally, with respect to intervention, domestic violence is defined in an attempt to connect domestic violence research to criminal justice responses. Given that the extant research and literature is from this perspective, this paper will examine domestic physical abuse perpetrated by women against their male partners.

DOMESTIC VIOLENCE COMMITTED BY MEN AGAINST WOMEN

Before engaging in a discussion of domestic violence perpetrated by women against men, we want to highlight the fact that there appears to be little dissension within the literature that "women, on average, suffer more frequent and more severe injury (physical, economic, and psychological)" than men as a result of domestic violence (Straus, in press, p. 4). Furthermore, a minority of women experience extreme, repetitive and systemic wife battering; to which men are unlikely to be exposed (Jasinski & Williams, 1998). This occurs to about 8% of women (Dutton, 1995).

DOMESTIC VIOLENCE COMMITTED BY WOMEN AGAINST MEN

Despite the fact that the domestic assault of men received scant attention until the 1990s, the prevalence of violence committed by women against male intimates has long been recognized. As early as the 1970s Straus and colleagues (1977-78) (see also: Steinmetz, 1978; Straus et al., 1980) reported that the results of the first National Family Violence Survey (NFVS; Straus et al., 1980) indicated that women inflicted physical assaults against male partners at a rate equivalent to the rate of male inflicted assaults against female partners. Since that time there has been a twenty-year controversy which Straus (in press) claimed had finally begun to subside by 1997. Straus (in press) hypothesized that the debate may have diminished due in large part to the rapidly expanding literature to support the NFVSs' results, indicating approximately equivalent rates of violence by men and women in cohabitating and marital relationships. Fiebert's (1997) annotated bibliography of 70 studies and Archer's meta-analysis further bolstered this position. Their reviews of the research demonstrated that "women are as physically aggressive, or more aggressive, than men in their relationships" (Fiebert, 1997, p. 273). However, Straus (in press) proposed that the gender debate was reignited by the recent release of the results of the National Violence Against Women Survey (NVAWS; Tjaden & Thoennes, 1998). The following section will examine briefly what has become a vast literature on female violence against male intimates. Unfortunately, a comprehensive review is not possible, but a discussion of various populations (e.g., national surveys, criminal victimization surveys, surveys of clinical and shelter populations, and dating violence literature) will provide an overview of the research to date.

NATIONAL SURVEYS AND THE GENERAL POPULATION

Perhaps the strongest evidence for concluding that women engage in comparable rates of domestic violence comes from national surveys of the general population, and primarily from the National Family Violence Surveys (NFVSs) in 1975 and 1985. The first NFVS (Straus, 1977-78; Straus et al., 1980) evidenced that in a given year women perpetrated more assaults (Median: males = 2.5 assaults/year; females = 3.0 assaults/year; Mean: males = 8.8 assaults/year; females = 10.1 assaults/year) and more severe assaults (Median: males = 2.4 severe assaults/year; females = 3.0 severe assaults/year; Mean: males = 8.0 severe assaults/year; females = 8.9 severe assaults/year) than men.

In 1985, Straus and Gelles replicated the NFVSs from the previous decade (Straus & Gelles, 1986). In these nationally representative samples of 2,143 (1975) and 6,002 (1985) married and co-habitating couples, Straus and Gelles (1986, 1990; Gelles & Straus, 1988) found that the rate of assaults by women against men was comparable, or slightly higher, than the rate of assaults by men against women. Because these data have been discussed extensively by the authors (see Gelles & Straus, 1988; Straus, 1993; Straus & Gelles, 1986, 1990) and by others (see Cook, 1997; Dutton, 1998) only a brief review of the results will be presented here. Slightly more than 16% of American couples reported a physical assault some time during 1985. Most of those assaults were random, although 3% of American women reported severe assaults. The NFVSs concluded that: (1) the rates of husband-to-wife and wife-to-husband abuse were almost equivalent; (2) the rate of wife beating decreased from 1975 to 1985, while the rate of husband beating remained fairly static; and, (3) the rate of severe domestic violence in the general population was relatively low. It should be noted that the NFVSs are the only nationally representative studies of family violence (Straus, 1990c). Based on NFVS data Cazaneave and Straus (1991) established the following class and race rates for severe husband assault: white/white collar 3%, white/blue collar 4%; black/white collar 3%, black/blue collar 9%. Hence, race and class appear to interact in influencing rates, white collar rates are identical by race. For severe wife assault, the rates were white/white collar 3%, white/blue collar 4%; black/white collar 7%, black/blue collar 8%. Wife assault appears to vary more by race, while husband assault varies more by class.

Given the heated debate that ensued following the publication of the controversial findings from the NFVS, Stets and Straus (1990) re-examined the data that indicated that women and men engaged in comparable rates of domestic assaults. Using a subset of 825 respondents who reported experiencing at least one or more assaults, Stets and Straus (1990) found that in half (49%) of the incidents the couples reported reciprocal violence. In 1/4 (23%) of the cases, the couples reported that the husband was violent and 1/4 (28%) of respondents reported that the wife was violent. Men (N = 297) reported striking the first blow in 43.7% of cases and that their partner struck the first blow in 44.1% of the cases (UK = 12.2%). The women (N = 428) reported striking the first blow in 52.7% of the cases and that their partner struck first blow in 42.6% of the cases (UK = 4.7%). Stets and Straus (1990) concluded that compared to the men, not only were the women in this sample equally likely to engage in violence, they were equally likely to instigate violence. The results also indicated that the women (24.4%) were more likely than the men (15%) to hit back in response to violent provocation by a partner.

Criticism of the NFVSs included the claim that violence by men and women is different because women are more likely to experience severe violence and, as a result, they are more likely to suffer injuries. The Stets and Straus (1990) data support these claims in part. Women (4.4%) reported that they engaged in severe violence as often as men (4.7%), although women (7.3%) who experienced severe assaults were more likely to need medical attention than men (1%) who experienced severe assaults. The results of Archer's (in press) meta-analysis provided further evidence that women are at greater risk of physical injury as a result of domestic violence. Archer (in press) reported that mean weighted (the mean effect size weighted by the sample size) values for the sex differences in sustained injuries and injuries requiring medical treatment both indicated that significantly more women than men were injured as a result of domestic abuse. However, it should be recalled that the vast majority of violence is of a "minor" nature. Of the men and women who reported suffering minor assaults on the NFVSs none of the women and less than 0.1% of the men needed to see a doctor (Stets & Straus, 1990).

Further criticism leveled at the NFVSs purported that there was a gender bias in the reporting. In 1993, Straus reanalyzed the data from the NFVSs to compare the rates in the general survey to the rates reported by women. Re-analysis of the data evidenced that women reported assaulting their husbands at a rate equivalent to what the men reported. Further support indicating that near equivalent rates of husband assault cannot be attributed to self-report bias is available from Archer's (in press) meta-analysis. According to self-reports, Archer (in press) found that women are more likely than men to commit acts of physical aggression; whereas, according to partner reports, their respective levels of abuse are similar. Archer concluded this is attributable to the outliers.

In addition to the first NFVS (Straus, 1977-78; Straus et al., 1980), several other pioneering studies concluded that men and women in the general population engage in comparable rates of domestic violence. Much of this early research can also be attributed with uncovering and reporting the existence of reciprocal abuse. Steinmetz (1977) examined the conflict tactics of 57 families selected from a public polling firm. Sixty-percent of the couples had reportedly used physical violence at least once during a conflict. Steinmetz reported there were few sex differences in the type and frequency of aggression, and many couples engaged in reciprocal aggression. Men and women were equally likely to have struck their spouse (20%) and to have hit their spouse with a hard object (10%) (Steinmetz, 1977). Scanzoni (1978) reported that 16% of the 321 women in this study reported attempting to strike their male partner when the couple was engaged in conflict. Nisonoff and Bitman (1979) found that of 297 questionnaires completed from a telephone survey men and women reported perpetrating (men = 15.5%; women = 11.3%) and being the target (men = 18.6%; women = 12.7%) of comparable rates of spouse abuse.

Although critics of the NFVSs purport that bias in the CTS is responsible for the nearly equivalent rates of male and female perpetrated abuse, studies using the CTS in independent samples drawn from the general population, as well as studies using other methods of measuring domestic violence, have provided further evidence of the validity of these results. Bland and Orn (1986) interviewed 1,200 (489 men; 711 women) randomly selected non-institutionalized Edmonton, Alberta residents using a standardized diagnostic interview. Results indicated that a significantly greater proportion of women (22.6%) than men (14.6%) reported ever hitting or throwing things at their spouse (X^2 = 8.4, p < .005). Women (73.4%) also reported that they were more likely than men (57.7%) to be the one who hit or threw things first. In another Canadian study, Lupri (1990, as cited in Cook, 1997) surveyed 1,123 men and women using a modified version of the CTS. Again, men (2.5%) were less likely to report having "beaten up" on their partners than women (6.2%); men were less likely (18%) to report aggressive acts in general than women (23%); and men reported committing fewer acts of serious aggression (10%) than women (13%). Using the CTS in a sample of 562 Canadian couples, Brinker- hoff and Lupri (1988) found women (10.7%) were twice as likely as men (4.8%) to use severe violence. Zlotnick, Kohn, Peterson and Pearstein (1998) analyzed data from 5,474 couples sampled in the National Survey of Families and Households and found nearly identical rates of assaults by men (5%) and women (4%).

Community surveys suggest that a significant minority of North American couples are involved in combative relationships with their spouse and that many of those are mutually abusive. Furthermore, the research suggests that a significant number of both men and women are at risk of being physically assaulted and that serious assaults are experienced by victims of both sexes; although women are more likely to be injured than men. We turn now to a discussion of the second major source of spouse abuse data, crime victimization surveys.

CRIME VICTIMIZATION SURVEYS

Crime victimization surveys suggest that the rate of domestic violence is a fraction of what conflict tactics surveys report and that female victims outnumber male victims of domestic violence by a large margin. The National Crime Survey (NCS; U.S. Department of Justice, 1980; Gaquin, 1977) and the National Crime Victimization Survey (the NCVS is a revision of the NCS; Bachman & Saltzman, 1995; Craven, 1994), the Canadian Urban Victimization Survey (CUVS; Solicitor General of Canada, 1985, see Johnson, 1988), the Canadian Violence Against Women Survey (VAWS; Rodgers, 1994) and the National Violence Against Women Survey (NVAW; Tjaden & Thoennes, 1998) report rates of domestic violence that range from 1/80th (NCS) to 1/12th (NVAW) of the rate of domestic violence uncovered by family conflict studies (Straus, in press). Crime victimization surveys also suggest that the proportion of women who assault men is a small fraction of the number of men who assault women. The male to female ratio reported in criminal victimization surveys ranges from 13 to 1 (NCS) to 3 to 1 (NVAWS), in contrast to the 1 to 1 ratio reported by family conflict studies.[1]

The discrepancies noted between crime victimization surveys and conflict tactic surveys have served to fuel the domestic violence debate. Crime victimization surveys ask respondents by what crimes they have been victimized. In contrast, conflict tactics surveys ask the respondent what type of actions they and their partner use to resolve conflict. Direct comparisons of the data derived from the two families of research can, therefore, be misleading.

Crime surveys are uniformly criticized for the influence of demand characteristics (Dutton, 1998; Straus, in press). Criminal victimization surveys are presented in the context of a "crime" survey; therefore, the respondent must label the assault a crime before they would report it. Research suggests that unless a domestic assault resulted in rare/extreme circumstances (i.e., such as injury) it is unlikely to be labeled a crime (for a discussion see Straus, in press). Dutton (1998) noted, for example, that the proportion of domestic assaults reported to police in crime victimization surveys (CUVS = 37%; NCS = 55%) is comparable to the proportion of other assaults reported to police. In contrast, the proportion of serious assaults (classified according to the CTS) reported to police in CTS studies is less than half (14.5%, see Schulman, 1979; Straus & Gelles, 1986) (Dutton, 1998). Dutton hypothesized this discrepancy might be accounted for by the fact that interspousal assaults are less likely to be considered a crime by the victim. If respondents are more likely to report serious assaults on crime surveys, Straus (in press) proposed that this would also account for the inflated rate of injury found in crime surveys (NCS = 75%; NCVS = 52%) compared to family conflict studies (3%).

Straus (in press) proposed that the same processes that result in discrepancies between the rate of domestic violence reported in crime surveys versus conflict tactics surveys (discussed briefly above) are likely to also account for the discrepancies in the ratio of male to female offenders reported by the two families of studies. If the "demand characteristics" of crime surveys result in respondents reporting predominantly assaults that culminate in injury, it follows that assaults by women are less likely to be reported (i.e., because women are more likely than men to be injured). Several authors argue that crime surveys likely underestimate the prevalence of "minor" assaults (Dutton, 1998; Straus, in press). Mihalic and Eilliot (1997) found that when inter-partner aggression is characterized as "criminal assault" as opposed to "relationship questions" respondents underreport abuse by 40%-83%. Straus further hypothesized that demand characteristics may also result in men being reluctant to report domestic assaults due to embarrassment or shame (i.e., men might not want to admit they were "afraid" of their partner) or because they may be less threatened by their partner than a woman would be and, therefore, even less likely to consider the domestic assault a crime. Archer (in press) also noted that crime surveys may involve interviewing the couple together, further confounding the results.

In addition to the data derived from national surveys and research with the general population and criminal victimization surveys, much of what we know about spouse abuse has been gleaned from research conducted with women sampled from clinical populations and shelters. This third family of domestic abuse research is discussed below.

CLINICAL AND SHELTER SAMPLES

Much of the early work on the prevalence and impact of domestic violence came from case studies and qualitative analyses of case studies from battered women in shelters (Dobash & Dobash, 1979; Pizzey, 1974; Walker, 1979). More often than not, clinical data indicated that males were the frequent and sole instigator of extreme and repetitive violence (see Dobash & Dobash, 1979; Giles-Sims, 1983; Pagelow, 1981; Walker, 1984). Straus (1993) critiqued the extant clinical data for neglecting to survey abused women regarding their own violence. In one of the few studies to examine abuse perpetrated by women sampled from a shelter, Pizzey (1974; 1982; see Thomas, 1993) reported that of 100 women 62% reported being violent toward their partners in addition to having been abused.

Critics of the CTS and those who are opposed to recognizing female batterers and male victims have been critical of the discrepancies noted between community surveys and clinical/shelter samples. Straus (1993) argued persuasively that research using clinical, shelter, and criminal justice data in addition to representative community surveys is necessary and that the results, despite being discrepant, are both correct.

The picture of domestic violence is likely to be characterized by two types of abusive couples (Johnson, 1995). The first, drawn from the general population and depicted in national surveys are composed of partners who experience mutual abuse of a more "minor" form. The second consists of individuals sampled from clinical populations and shelters and are comprised of women who are the victims of repeated, serious abuse by their partner. Johnson (1995) hypothesized that most violence engaged in by these women would be characterized as self-defense. Further evidence that these are unique populations can be drawn from Johnson's (1995) research that suggests reciprocal aggression is commonly found in community samples, in contrast to male inflicted assaults which are more prevalent in clinical samples (see O'Leary et al., 1989).

Johnson's (1995) examination of domestic abuse in clinical versus community samples led her to conclude that the results obtained from domestic violence research invariably reflect differences in the population from which the samples are taken. Generalizations about abused wives in general made based on information derived from clinical samples results in what is known as the "clinical fallacy"; (i.e., over-generalizing the results of a clinical sample to the general population) and comparably, generalizations about victims of severe violence made based on information derived from community samples results in the "representative sample fallacy" (Straus, 1993; see also Johnson, 1995; Straus, 1990b). Discrepancies between community surveys and research with samples of women from clinical/shelter populations can be attributed to self-report and self-selection biases.

Archer (in press) contends that clinical studies are plagued by self-report biases. "Partner reports for the men are being compared with self-reports for the women" (p. 14), resulting in an unavoidable bias. Archer's (1999a) meta-analysis demonstrated that self-reports reflect lower assault rates than partner reports.

McNeely and Robinson-Simpson (1987) critiqued the fact that much of the literature on domestic violence, and the conclusions drawn from there, are based on clinical populations of battered women who have sought mental health interventions or entered women's shelters. Clinical/shelter victims may differ significantly from women who do not present for treatment or who report the assault to police (e.g., they may have been victim to more severe and/or repeated violence) (McNeely & Robinson-Simpson, 1987). In an attempt to reconcile the discrepancies in the research Stets and Straus (1990) note that this is consistent with other research, on depression and alcoholism for instance, where the "treatment populations differ in important ways from non-treatment populations" (Stets & Straus, 1990, p. 164). McNeely and Robinson-Simpson (1987) proposed that research conclusions drawn from clinical samples should not be used to draw conclusions about domestic violence generally. Rather, their primary benefit is to inform about treatment. Specifically, Straus (1990) proposed that research using clinical samples and police records only provide information about 1% of battered women (i.e., the percentage of assaults resulting in arrest according to the 1985 NFVS).

A review of the domestic violence research from clinical populations and shelters suggests three general conclusions: (1) Research is needed to explore the incidence and prevalence of women's aggression, reciprocal abuse, and aggression used in self-defense in clinical and refuge populations; (2) Data from studies using refuge and clinical samples of women are important to our understanding of domestic violence generally, and severe wife battering specifically, but should be considered with an appreciation that they do not necessarily reflect the experiences of women from the general population; and, (3) Results from such studies should be tempered with an appreciation of the effect of self-report biases.

DATING VIOLENCE

Makepeace (1981) was the pioneer who first reported that violence in dating relationships is as rampant as it is in cohabitating and marital relationships. Makepeace (1986) critiqued the extant literature, stating that small sample sizes may have contributed to findings of inconsistent gender victimization and perpetration results. He argued that due to variation in the operationalization of victimization and small sample sizes, many studies have not differentiated the reports of aggression by sex. In an attempt to address his criticisms Makepeace (1986) analyzed reports of the worst incident in the responses of a subsample of 391 undergraduates who reported experiencing dating violence. Females (20.6%) reported experiencing more dating violence than males (12%), although the mean number of experiences did not differ by sex (3.50 vs. 3.54). Males (26.8%) reported being aggressors three times more often than females (8.6%); and females (72.9%) were more likely than males (41.2%) to report being the target of dating violence. However, Makepeace (1986) noted that the majority of males and females considered themselves to be the victim or the cobelligerent, and high numbers of males (27.7%) and females (22.9%) reported that the other party was responsible for initiating violence. Makepeace (1986) also examined the respondents' perception of effects by gender. Females reported sustaining three times as much mild physical injury, and twice as much moderate and severe physical injury as males.

Following Makepeace's groundbreaking research several studies have examined dating violence (see Fiebert, 1997). In many ways the dating violence literature mirrors the spouse abuse literature. There appears to be a split in the literature, with some studies reporting that women are more likely than men to be victimized in a dating relationship (Makepeace, 1981, 1986; Simonelli & Ingram, 1998), but many researchers have concluded that there is a large proportion of dating couples who are reciprocally assaultive (Bernard & Bernard, 1983; Burke, Stets and Pirog-Good, 1988; Henton, Cate, Koval, Lloyd, & Christopher, 1983; Stets & Pirog-Good, 1987). And, in some cases, the data suggest that a higher proportion of females than males are violent against dates (Majdan, 1998; O'Keefe, Brockopp, & Chew, 1986; Sugarman & Hotaling, 1989; Thompson, 1991).

A review of the dating violence literature indicates that there is sufficient empirical evidence indicating the incidence, prevalence and severity of aggression by both men and women in dating relationships warrants concern. Of particular import, there is clear evidence that men comprise a significant proportion of the victims of dating violence. In addition, the body of literature on dating violence is consistent with what we reported from the domestic abuse literature: That many couples engage in mutual combat.

CONCLUSION

In his recent meta-analytic review of aggression in heterosexual relationships, Archer (in press) concluded that women were more likely to use physical aggression and to use it more often than men; however, men were more likely to injure their partners. Hampton and colleagues noted that despite the apparent prevalence of domestic violence against men there are virtually no social policies or programs in place to address the needs of male victims (Hampton et al., 1989). This has not changed dramatically in the last decade. We propose that social service providers are doing female perpetrators, male victims, and their children a disservice by neglecting the "other side of domestic abuse." The serious physical, psychological, and social implications of domestic abuse, regardless of the sex of the victim of the perpetrator, requires an abrupt turn-about by the academic community, law enforcement and policy makers alike. We propose that recognition of the need for prevention, identification, and intervention for both male and female victims and perpetrators should be one of the mental health initiatives for the new millennium.

The empirical research reviewed in this paper, although admittedly incomplete, suggests that reciprocal abuse does exist, but that the prevalence of mutual abuse is difficult to ascertain from the research to date. For instance, simply asking respondents if they have both assaulted, and been assaulted by, their partner does not provide enough information to ascertain if the data reflect mutual abuse, retaliatory aggression on rare occasions, or self-defense. Clearly, this is a political hotbed, but the information could provide data to enlighten our archaic propensity to treat male batterers and female victims, and ignore the needs of female batterers and male victims.

Our review of the extant literature supports several tenuous conclusions: (1) the majority of domestic violence is between two combative individuals who are both in need of therapeutic intervention; (2) women are as likely to aggress against partners as are men, and men are as likely as women to be the victims of domestic assaults; (3) women are more likely to be physically injured as a result of domestic violence; and finally, (4) the male "batterer" who repeatedly, systematically and severely abuses his wife is unfortunately a reality, but thankfully, a fairly rare one (Dutton, 1998).

NOTE

1. It is debatable whether the NVAWS should be classified as a crime victimization survey. The survey is not presented to respondents as a survey of their criminal victimization histories and would not, therefore, be plagued by to the same degree by the demand characteristics crime victimization surveys encounter. It should also be noted that the section of the study pertaining to physical assaults used a modified version of the CTS (Straus, 1979). These two differences likely account for the fact that the results of this study more closely resemble those of conflict tactics studies. However, see Straus (in press, 1998) for a discussion of the effect of the context on the NVAWS results. The NVAWS is used here as a comparison to avoid overstating the discrepancies between the results of CTS studies and other surveys of national samples.

REFERENCES

Archer, J. (in press). An assessment of the reliability of the Conflict Tactics Scale: A meta-analytic review. *Journal of Interpersonal Violence.*

Archer, J. (in press). Sex differences in aggression between heterosexual partners: A meta-analytic review. *Psychological Review.*

Bachman, R. & Saltzman, L. E. (1995). *Violence against women: Estimates from the redesigned survey* (BJS Publication No. 154-348). Washington, DC: U.S. Department of Justice, Bureau of Justice Statistics.

Bernard, M. L., & Bernard, J. L. (1983, April). Violent intimacy: The family as a model for love relationships. *Family Relations,* 32, 283-286.

Bland, R., & Orn, H. (1986). Family violence and psychiatric disorder. *Canadian Journal of Psychiatry, 31,* (2), 129-137.

Burke, P. J., Stets, J. E., & Pirog-Good, M. A. (1988). Gender identity, self-esteem, and physical and sexual abuse in dating relationships. *Social Psychology Quarterly, 51,* 272-285.

Cazaneave, N. A., & Straus, M. A. (1991). Race, class, social embeddedness and family violence: A search for potent support systems. In M. A. Straus & R. J. Gelles (Eds.), *Physical Violence in American Families* (pp. 321-336). Transaction Publishers: New Brunswick, NJ.

Cook, P. W. (1998). *Abuse men: The hidden side of domestic violence.* Westport, CT: Praeger.

Craven, D. (1994). *Sex differences in violent victimization.* Special Report, Washington, DC: U.S. Department of Justice, Bureau of Justice Statistics, September, 1997, NCJ 164508.

Dobash, R., & Dobash, R. (1979). *Violence against wives.* New York: Free Press.

Dutton, D. G. (1998). *The domestic assault of women: Psychological and criminal justice perspectives.* Vancouver, BC: U.B.C. Press.

Fiebert, M. S. (1997). Annotated bibliography: References examining assaults by women on their spouses/partners. In B. M. Dank & R. Refinette (Eds.), *Sexual harassment & sexual consent* (Vol. 1, pp. 273-286). New Brunswick: Transaction Publishers.

Gaquin, D. A. (1977). Spouse abuse: Data from the National Crime Survey. *Victimology, 2* (3-4), 632-642.

Gelles, R. J. & Straus, M. A. (1988). *Intimate violence.* New York, NY: Simon & Schuster.

Giles-Sims, J. (1983). *Wife-battering: A systems theory approach.* New York: Guilford Press.

Hampton, R. L., Gelles, R. J., & Harrop, J. W. (1989). Is violence in black families increasing?: A comparison of 1975 and 1985 national survey rates. *Journal of Marriage and the Family, 51,* 969-980.

Henton, J., Cate, R., Koval, J., Lloyd, S., & Christopher, S. (1983). Romance and violence in dating relationships. *Journal of Family Issues, 4,* 467-482.

Hotaling, G. T., Straus, M. A., & Lincoln, A. J. (1990). Intrafamily violence and crime and violence outside the family. In M. A. Straus & R. J. Gelles (Eds.), *Physical violence in American families.* New Brunswick, NJ: Transaction Publishers.

Jasinski, J. L., & Williams, L. M. (Eds.) (1998). *Partner violence: A comprehensive review of 20 years of research.* Thousand Oaks, CA: Sage.

Johnson, H. (1988, Spring). Wife abuse. *Canadian Social Trends (Statistics Canada),* 17-20.

Johnson, M. P. (1995). Patriarchal terrorism and common couple violence: Two forms of violence against women. *Journal of Marriage and the Family, 57,* 283-294.

Majdan, A. (1998). *Prevalence and personality correlates of women's aggression against male partners.* Unpublished master's thesis. Simon Fraser University, Vancouver, BC, Canada.

Makepeace, J. (1981). Courtship violence among college students. *Family Relations, 30,* 97-102.

Makepeace, J. (1986, July). Gender differences in courtship violence victimization. *Family Relations,* 35, 383-388.

McNeely, R. L., & Robinson-Simpson, G. (1987, November-December). The truth about domestic violence: A falsely framed issue. *Social Work,* 32, 485-490.

Mihalic, S. W. & Elliott, D. (1997). If violence is domestic, does it really count? *Journal of Family Violence, 12,* 293-311.

Nisonoff, L., & Bitman, I. (1979). Spouse abuse: Incidence and relationship to selected demographic variables. *Victimology, 4,* 131-140.

O'Leary, K. D., Barling, J., Arias, I., Rosenbaum, A., Malone, J., & Tyree, A. (1989). Prevalence and stability of physical aggression. *Journal of Consulting and Clinical Psychology, 57,* 263-268.

Pagelow, M. D. (1981). *Woman-battering: Victims and their experiences.* Newbury Park, CA: Sage.

Pizzey, E. (1974). *Scream quietly or the neighbors will hear.* London: Penquin.

Pizzey, E. (1982). *Prone to Violence.* Prone to violence. Ottawa, Canada: Commoners' Publishing.

Rodgers, K. (1994, Autumn). Wife assault in Canada. *Canadian Social Trends* (Statistics Canada), 3-8.

Scanzoni, J. (1978). *Sex roles, women's work, and marital conflict.* Lexington, MA: Lexington.

Schulman, M. (1979). *A survey of spousal violence against women in Kentucky.* Washington, DC: US Department of Justice, Law Enforcement.

Simonelli, C. J., & Ingram, K. M. (1998). Psychological distress among men experiencing physical and emotional abuse in heterosexual dating relationships. *Journal of Interpersonal Violence, 13,* 667-672.

Solicitor General of Canada (1985). Canadian Urban Victimization Survey. *Female Victims of Crime.* Bulletin no. 4. Ottawa.

Steinmetz, S. K. (1977-78). The battered husband syndrome. *Victimology, 2,* 499-509.

Steinmetz, S. K. (1977). Wifebeating, husband-beating–A comparison of the use of physical force between spouses to resolve marital fights. In M. Roy (Ed.), *Battered Women.* New York: Van Nostrand.

Stets, J. E., & Pirog-Good, M. A. (1987). Violence in dating relationships. *Social Psychology Quarterly, 50,* 237-246.

Stets, J. E. & Straus, M. A. (1990). *Gender differences in reporting of marital violence and its medical and psychological consequences.* In M. A. Straus & R. J. Gelles (Eds.), Physical violence in American families: Risk factors and adaptations to violence in 8,145 families (pp. 151-165). New Brunswick, NJ: Transaction.

Straus, M. (1977-78). Wife-beating: How common and why? *Victimology, 2,* 443-458.

Straus, M. (1990b). Injury and frequency of assault and the representative sample fallacy in measuring wife beating and child abuse. In M. A. Straus and R. J. Gelles

(Eds.), *Physical violence in American families: Risk factors and adaptations to violence in 8,145 families* (pp. 75-91). New Brunswick, NJ: Transaction Books.

Straus, M. (1990c). The national family violence surveys. In M. A. Straus and R. J. Gelles (Eds.), *Physical violence in American families: Risk factors and adaptations to violence in 8,145 families* (pp. 3-16). New Brunswick, NJ: Transaction Books.

Straus, M. (1993). Physical assaults by wives: A major social problem. In R. J. Gelles & D. R. Loseke (Eds.), *Current controversies on family violence* (pp. 67-87). Newbury, CA: Sage.

Straus, M. (in press). The controversy over domestic violence by women: A methodological, theoretical, and sociology of science analysis. To appear in X. B. Arriaga & S. Oskamp (Eds.), *Violence in intimate relationships.* Thousand Oaks, CA: Sage.

Straus, M., & Gelles, R. J. (1986). Societal change and change in family violence from 1975 to 1985 as revealed by two national surveys. *Journal of Marriage & the Family, 48,* 465-479.

Straus, M., & Gelles, R. J. (Eds.). (1990). *Violence in American families: Risk factors and adaptations to violence in 8,145 families.* New Brunswick, NJ: Transaction Publishers.

Straus, M. A., Gelles, R. J., & Steinmetz, S. (1980). *Behind closed doors: Violence in the American family.* Garden City, NY: Anchor/Doubleday.

Straus, M. A. & Sweet, S. (1992). Verbal/symbolic aggression in couples: Incidence rates and relationships to personal characteristics. *Journal of Marriage and the Family, 54,* 346-357.

Sugarman, D. B., & Hotaling, G. T. (1989). Dating violence: Prevalence, context, and risk markers. In A. A. Pirog-Good & J. E. Stets (Eds.), *Violence in dating relationships: Emerging Social Issues* (pp. 3-31). New York: Praeger.

Thompson, E. H. (1991). The maleness of violence in dating relationships: An appraisal of stereotypes. *Sex Roles, 24,* 261-278.

Tjaden, P., & Thoennes, N. (1998, November). Prevalence, incidence, and consequences of violence against women: Findings from the National Violence Against Women Survey. U.S. Department of Justice, National Institute of Justice. Taken from NIJ's Web site http://www.ofp.usdoj.gov/nij

Vissing, Y. M., Straus, M. A., Gelles, R. J., & Harrop, J. W. (1993). Verbal aggression by parents and psychosocial problems of children. *Child Abuse and Neglect, 15,* 223-238.

Walker, L. E. (1979). *The battered woman.* New York: Harper & Row.

Walker, L. W. (1984). *The battered woman syndrome.* New York: Springer.

Zlotnick, C., Kosh, R., Peterson, J., & Pearlstein, T. (1998). Partner physical victimization in a National Sample of American families: Relationship to psychological functioning, psychosocial factors, and gender. *Journal of Interpersonal Violence, 13* (1), 156-166.

Men Helping Boys Become Men

Norman Shub

SUMMARY. This paper explores the idea of men raising boys to be men as a potential site for abuse in the rearing of men and then creating abusive men. Looking at issues such as character building, the use of symbols to connote power and authority, and corporal punishment to create respect, the article, in a very personal way, explores the process of this segment of child rearing as a potential for creating abusive men in adulthood. *[Article copies available for a fee from The Haworth Document Delivery Service: 1-800-342-9678. E-mail address: <getinfo@haworthpressinc. com> Website: <http://www.HaworthPress.com> © 2001 by The Haworth Press, Inc. All rights reserved.]*

KEYWORDS. Abuse, being a man, fatherhood, limits

INTRODUCTION

The invitation to submit an article for this volume devoted to the topic "abuse of men" stimulated an enormous upheaval in my internal

---

Norman Shub, BCD, is an author, teacher, and psychotherapist. Known as a clear and articulate "master teacher," Norman's pioneering work in differential diagnosis, as well as the treatment of character disorders, is widely recognized. He is president of Gestalt Associates, Inc., a group psychotherapy practice, as well as its business consulting team, the Business of People organization. In addition to books and articles, Norman's current publications include *The Working Paper Series*, which is devoted to developing the effectiveness of the psychotherapist and the students of psychotherapy. He is married to Debbie and proud father of Ariel.

[Haworth co-indexing entry note]: "Men Helping Boys Become Men." Shub, Norman. Co-published simultaneously in *Journal of Couples Therapy* (The Haworth Press, Inc.) Vol. 10, No. 1, 2001, pp. 59-68; and: *The Abuse of Men: Trauma Begets Trauma* (ed: Barbara Jo Brothers) The Haworth Press, Inc., 2001, pp. 59-68. Single or multiple copies of this article are available for a fee from The Haworth Document Delivery Service [1-800-342-9678, 9:00 a.m. - 5:00 p.m. (EST). E-mail address: getinfo@haworthpressinc. com].

landscape. It encouraged me to consider an issue that I have long avoided writing about, although I have always wanted to. I have, however, worked on this issue intensively in my own therapy, dealt with it in many clients, and struggled with its countertransference problems. I have often thought about it during my time as a mental health professional. That issue, which I want to address here, is the abuse that may occur when men teach boys how to be men, words I write somewhat ironically. The issue is important for me because of my own father's attempts to shape me into his stereotyped concept of what a man is supposed to be. These attempts impacted me in ways of which he had no conception.

Perhaps most importantly, writing this article has helped me to redefine as truly abusive some of the methods my father employed and that many other fathers have employed in their attempts to make their children Men. Although I have struggled with the impact of my youthful experiences, writing about them in terms of abuse is a new–and a painfully upsetting–experience for me. Tears have come to my eyes as I have written and as I have relived difficult memories of the man-shaping process and thought about how hard I have worked to overcome the impact of my father's efforts to teach me to obey, to be a man, to buck up, and to take it.

DISCIPLINE VERSUS ABUSE

It is clear to me that, for me and for many other men, what was billed as discipline and performed in the name of discipline at times became abusive. My suffering and its consequences for me were overwhelming. From the age of four on, my memories of my father involve terrifying actions that would ensue when I did not comply exactly with what he wanted. He would begin to raise his voice and then would escalate toward a major confrontation. My every non-compliance from the age of four on, even to irrational and ridiculous demands, resulted in his striking out at me and acting out against me. If I contradicted my father, made a suggestion, or tried to hold him accountable for his promise to take my brother and me someplace, give us something, or do something for us, I was inevitably labeled disrespectful. Disrespect led to what he called "discipline," which he enforced to teach me to respect or listen to him or, in his words, to behave.

This discipline process, which occurred almost every day of my young life, culminated in a physical confrontation in which my father's methods taught me, at the age of thirteen, to become abusive in turn. I finally lost control. On my way home from school, I was supposed to purchase the exact list of products my father had requested the day before. That night, he quizzed me about whether I had bought the desired list. When it became clear that I had forgotten one item, he became angry. He yelled at me, told me that I did not respect him and never listened to him, and demanded to know what was wrong with me. As usual, this confrontation continued to escalate as he yelled violently about honoring and respecting one's father and pinched and hit me.

Something finally snapped in me. I lost control and, like a savage dog, I attacked my father and pounded him with my fists as I cried and screamed. It was a spasm of violence the like of which I had never experienced. I beat up my father. Then, as I began to calm down while sitting on top of him and sobbing, I became instantly terrified of what I had done. I looked him in the eye and silently begged him for forgiveness. I was terrified that something terrible had happened and that I had done something irrevocably damaging.

My father glared at me as I got up and looked at him beseechingly, hoping that he would say something kind or forgiving. Instead, he walked away without a word. That was it. The connection had snapped. From that time on, my heart was like ice when I thought of him. The cycle of abuse had now turned. He had abused me, and now I felt abusive toward him.

The picture of my father screaming about discipline, respect, and the biblical injunction to honor your father and mother while acting out at me is an emotional photographic that will never fade or turn brown and crinkle at the edges. It is as vivid to me today as it was during those years between four and thirteen when the daily fights occurred.

My mother was schizophrenic, and both my parents were concentration camp survivors. Schizophrenia was not well understood then, and it was probably rampant among those who survived the trauma of the camps. My father would become angry at my mother for her craziness, and, if the nightly fights did not concern me, then they probably started over something she had done. If I challenged his brutality to her or cried or yelled, he would discipline me to teach me boundaries and limits. When my father was in a bad mood, he would find something to get angry about and then would pick a fight. In my case, such fights always escalated. I would fight back and become outraged.

My brother hated the conflicts and would yell at me to stop it. He blamed me for egging my father on and tried to be the family broker or mediator to stop the conflicts. I would become enraged, and we would go toe to toe. This led to my father chasing me around the house or outdoors with a broom, kicking me, and throwing me on the floor. His purpose was to shut me up and teach me respect, to discipline me so that I would behave. The end result was the story I related above.

In our immigrant neighborhood, my father's behavior was seen as mean spirited but not abusive. Other fathers hit their boys repeatedly, and a belief in the BELT was common. Men pulling off their straps and belts to whack their children was a reality that everyone in the neighborhood experienced in one way or another.

The significant point is that clearly abusive behaviors were, at that point in my development, named as discipline and seen as part of what was necessary to make me a man. I have seen the same pattern in the lives of many clients raised by fathers who thought that such methods would help shape up their sons, teach them boundaries and respect, and show them where they ended and the world began. Such methods are frequently conceptualized as part of a family's discipline.

My mother never really rebelled, nor did my relatives or neighbors who witnessed my father's treatment of me. Only in extreme cases, when he would kick me repeatedly or get me down on the ground and keep hitting me, would they stop the escalating brutality. Most people were philosophically opposed to complaining or saying anything. Other fathers acted similarly, and their methods were considered an aspect of raising children. To this day, I observe clients, relatives, and friends place what I consider to be clearly abusive behaviors in a disciplinary framework.

Physical discipline through beatings and other brutalities never helped me experience a boundary, internalize a value, or give respect. Corporal punishment as a tactic under the rubric of discipline never achieved the effect desired by my father and uncle, the neighborhood men, and other fathers I have known and seen. Their methodology did not achieve their goals.

BUILDING CHARACTER

My father and the neighborhood men believed that physically disciplining their children helped build character. What they meant by that, as I have heard from many men and fathers, is that such discipline makes sons (and daughters) tough after they learn they can take it. It builds character, strengthens them, and helps them develop the ramrod toughness needed to cope with the world.

The philosophy that physical discipline and punishment help toughen us is true, but not in the way that my father perceived it. My father's hitting me did not strengthen me in my ability to deal with the world or make me characterologically stronger. Rather, it promoted characterologic rigidity. People with healthy characters display much flexibility, particularly in terms of their core traits, and possess many behavioral options.

The physicality that my father thought would build my character actually helped narrow it and limit my options, however. I did not learn various ways of dealing with anger. I did not learn how to say how I felt, to complain, to respond, to get angry appropriately, or to say my words. On the one hand, I learned to clamp down on my anger by locking my jaw, tightening myself, and expressing nothing while thinking that I would be damned if I let him see my vulnerability. On the other hand, I learned to express my rage and temper in a massively out-of-control manner.

The physicality that my father called discipline actually narrowed my character. Rather than strengthening me, it limited my options for dealing with the external environment. It pushed me into the characterologically repetitive behavior that became part of my characterologic problem later in life.

This idea among men who raise boys that physically disciplining and dominating them will toughen them and build their character usually has the opposite result. It creates rigid characterologic formulations that make adult life more difficult, as the question of honesty illustrates.

When confronted with an honesty issue, my father would begin yelling at me about telling the truth. I did not learn various options through patient, gentle, loving work. I did not learn to say the truth, to say that I was afraid to tell the truth, to tell him a difficulty of which I was ashamed, to say I had lied or told a half truth, or to say that I could not talk about that subject right then. I was not taught the skills or given the time to run to my room and hide, which might have allowed me to build up my courage to tell my father on my own that something was wrong or to realize that deceit was not the option I wanted to choose.

On the honesty/dishonesty continuum, my father did not use support, patience, tenderness, and involvement to teach me how to enjoy many characterologic options. Rather, the minute he sensed dishonesty, he would yell at me. I would rigidify and would either lie or shut up. Eventually my behavioral options narrowed further as I learned to either lie or say nothing in the face of mounting hostility. Nevertheless, many men, supported by ideas found in literature, television, and movies, continue to believe that this approach actually strengthens character. It does not.

THAT'S IT:
LIMIT SETTING

Another aspect of the abuse that constituted my father's idea of discipline was the idea that the way to delimit a boundary or set a limit was to say, "That's it, I've had enough," and then explode. Frequently my family would be eating a meal, debating, kidding around, or engaging in horseplay and my father would reach the edge of his own particular tolerance. He did not try to help us understand how and when this process occurred or to see when he was moving toward his boundary. He did not care whether his response was appropriate or whether my brother or I were at a boundary. He would shout, "That's it," and explode, punishing us because he was over his boundary.

My father believed that this response would teach me respect for his and other people's boundaries. However, I clearly experienced this behavior as abuse. It desensitized me to people's boundaries and taught me that a person could erupt at any moment and that doing so was OK when a boundary was reached. My father's abusive behavior had the opposite effect from what he intended. I did not learn to understand boundaries and what moving toward them feels like or how to respect limits and set boundaries. I learned to explode and act out when I reached a boundary. I did not learn to see or respect other adults or children. If I harassed them, joked with them, or teased them,

I could not see when I was pushing them too far to the edge of what they could tolerate.

So I grew up with little sense of boundaries and little understanding of how to respect my own or other people's. This ignorance, one consequence of which was my trouble managing my anger, manifested itself in difficulties in my marriage, with my child, with clients, with friends, and in various therapeutic and non-therapeutic relationships. In all of the ways that I interacted with others, I understood very little about boundaries or boundary sensitivity.

THE BELT, THE ROD, THE STICK, OR OTHER SYMBOLS OF AUTHORITY

The Belt as both object and metaphor for teaching limits and respect, for building character, and for signaling that something was going to happen was another abusive tactic used by my father, our neighbors, and many people I have encountered as a psychotherapist and citizen. Clearly, my father believed that endowing his belt (or you can substitute the principal's paddle or the cane of my friend's father) with a special significance would produce some sort of salutary effect in me or control over me when he waved it about or threatened to use it.

Again, creating this kind of metaphor or symbol and endowing it with what my father thought was authority and power but was actually violence profoundly impacted me in a negative way. Without any awareness, I found myself as a child in my latency years always wanting the whip, the stick, or the cane because for me, as for my father, they were symbols of power. I wanted to have authority. I wanted to be a big man. I often walked home from school with a stick that I poked and tapped with, played with, and sometimes hit people with. I was repeating my father's behavior and learning in my childlike way to begin the process of using my power symbol. By using my stick, which I considered an element of power, I was labeled as bad, because I did poke kids and hit them. This label justified my father waving his stick around and abusing me more as he tried to build my character and teach me respect and boundaries and how to be a good citizen.

The belt, the stick, and the cane created those kinds of experiences for me and taught me to see such objects as empowering. They also taught me violence as an aspect of the way one treats other people.

They taught me that waving around a stick was an acceptable way of exerting authority. This metaphor became extremely problematic for me as I grew up, however. Rather than understanding the respectful use of power and the importance of that process in human life, I thought that power was something you took or grabbed, not something that was earned and developed.

This misunderstanding has haunted me throughout my life. As I worked on this article, I realized that only recently, in my late forties and fifties, have I come to reject the idea of power as something you grab rather than as something that is given to you in an honorable way. It is with the deepest regret that I have worked hard to reverse the impact of this metaphor on my life.

OTHER IMPACTS

I have discussed some of the negative consequences to myself of the abusive disciplinary tactics that my father used. In addition to these major setbacks, I would like to identify some other negative impacts on young men who are abusively disciplined by one or both parents.

Tightening Up

I can remember vividly sitting at the kitchen or dining room table and watching my father usually, but sometimes my mother, start to get angry. During the first couple of years, I would stop breathing and become terrified. Then, as these episodes persisted and occurred almost daily, I would tighten up so that I would not cry, would not feel, and would not experience the screaming and physical pain that was coming. The consequences for me in terms of my development were horrendous and overwhelming.

Shutting Down My Feelings

As time passed, I became more out of touch with my feelings. In order to cope with the nightly fights and to show my father that I was tough, I cut my feelings off so that I did not feel, did not cry, and did not seem vulnerable or weak. I showed him that I was as tough as he was.

Well, we all know that emotions are not like light switches. Gradually I could not turn my feelings back on and off. Then, as an adolescent and an adult, I had such difficulty feeling my emotional self that I could not cry at movies, felt very little, and was unable to experience sensitivity and love. In order to survive, I had to shut myself down, and I paid a high price for that survival tactic.

Ineffective Ways of Managing Anger

Abusive discipline also taught me ineffective ways of managing my anger. In addition to cutting off my feelings, I tensed up. Tension and clenching my fists and tightening my jaw and stomach became for me a prelude to violence. I needed to release the internal tension I felt in order to regain my homeostatic balance as a person. I would release the tension by acting violently and screaming, yelling, hitting, kicking, and fighting back.

I learned to associate tension release with the expression of some kind of violence or anger, a poor lesson to say the least. I remember standing in my parents' living room and feeling the tension build up and then screaming to the point where I was almost foaming at the mouth. Then I see myself later as a newlywed, and my wife does something that really makes me angry. Again I remember screaming at her to the same almost-foaming-at-the-mouth point. I had no stops. I did not realize how out of control or abusive I was and how I was repeating the cycle that was implanted in me in the name of discipline.

Anxiety

In the early years, I became terrified, and the terror of always waiting for and anticipating my father to blow up preoccupied me and made me extremely anxious. Many children who are raised under abusive discipline develop anxiety about something bad happening. A boy raised in an environment where he is disciplined abusively every time something goes wrong obviously develops anxiety waiting for the bad thing to happen.

This anxiety manifested itself in my adult life in a constant anticipation and dread of something going wrong. A registered letter or a phone call from someone terrified me with thoughts of bad news. Through my own therapy and struggling to understand what had happened to me and how my father's violent discipline had affected me, I have been able to move somewhat beyond the fears that developed in my early years. They did profoundly affect me, however. Children who are raised under a discipline-abuse cycle often are terrified of something bad happening because, sooner or later, something bad does happen.

Strength Lies in Withholding

The final lesson I learned from the abuse cycle is that strength lies in withholding. I learned to grit my teeth and go on. I learned to rigidify. I learned to tighten down. I learned to hold back. I learned that the way to be strong and not show weakness, to demonstrate my power, and to not let my father see that he could get to me was by withholding emotion, feeling, pain, and expression.

This idea that strength consists of gritting one's teeth and going on rather than dealing with reality also hurt me in many ways as an adult. First, it made it difficult for me to manage conflict because I would withdraw, withhold, get angry, and tighten down. Second, it narrowed my character even further. Third, I really began to believe–and did so for a long time–that people's strength came from not dealing with things. Strength was toughening it out. In my marriage, in my friendships, in my therapy, and in other areas of my life, I misinterpreted strength for weakness. I made my own emotional world and other people's lives much more difficult because of this lesson I learned from the abusive discipline cycle.

CONCLUSION

By looking primarily in this article at my own experience with a father who employed extreme physical abuse in the name of discipline, I have hoped to demonstrate how discipline in raising male children particularly can create an abusive cycle. I hope that my experience can sensitize fathers and mothers, psychotherapists, and anyone who deals with abuse to expand their framework of abusive men and abused boys to conclude that some of the behaviors that many of us still regard positively–or at least not negatively–truly can be abusive and truly can have profoundly negative impacts on people's lives.

Intertraumatic Dissociative Attachment: Treating Trauma-Based Transactions in Couples

Erwin Randolph Parson

SUMMARY. This article focuses on the treatment of couples with a collective personal history of *multiple* traumatic experiences, and central related concepts. Referred to as the *intertrauma couples therapy* (InTCT) model, this article outlines an approach to treating trauma victim couples in which each partner has suffered one or more traumatic experiences (i.e., war, rape, criminal assault, incest, community violence, etc.). InTCT is a structured five-phase model of care, derived from a long trauma treatment tradition, and the author's clinical experience in the treatment of multitrauma persons for over 20 years.

This comprehensive, integrative approach to treatment is designed to resolve chronic interpersonal hostility, isolation in marriage, fears of intimacy and engulfment, and the persistent revivifications of partners' traumatic memories as a painful product of daily relational encounters. Unfortunately, these encounters represent *trauma structures interacting with trauma structures,* with no end or relief to the mutual pain-generating interactional patterns. The phases of the treatment takes the couple from disorganization and intense emotional reactivity to stabilization through integration to an end phase with a post-integration life skills building program for lasting results. Also presented are issues such as attachment, specific trauma responses to include interactive concepts of

Erwin Randolph Parson, PhD, is Leader, National PTSD/Mental Health Seminar, Veterans Annual Concerns Conference, Capitol Hill, Washington, DC, and is Trauma Psychologist/Consultant, VA Maryland Health Care System.

Address correspondence to: Erwin Randolph Parson, P.O. Box 55, Perry Point, MD 21902-0062.

[Haworth co-indexing entry note]: "Intertraumatic Dissociative Attachment: Treating Trauma-Based Transactions in Couples." Parson, Erwin Randolph. Co-published simultaneously in *Journal of Couples Therapy* (The Haworth Press, Inc.) Vol. 10, No. 1, 2001, pp. 69-112; and: *The Abuse of Men: Trauma Begets Trauma* (ed: Barbara Jo Brothers) The Haworth Press, Inc., 2001, pp. 69-112. Single or multiple copies of this article are available for a fee from The Haworth Document Delivery Service [1-800-342-9678, 9:00 a.m. - 5:00 p.m. (EST). E-mail address: getinfo@haworthpressinc.com].

69

trauma bonding and systems theory in the context of trauma and dissociation. The article also presents a multitrauma couple case study, and discusses the critical role of therapist's functions. *[Article copies available for a fee from The Haworth Document Delivery Service: 1-800- 342-9678. E-mail address: <getinfo@haworthpressinc.com> Website: <http://www.HaworthPress. com> © 2001 by The Haworth Press, Inc. All rights reserved.]*

KEYWORDS. Couple therapy, trauma, theory, biopsychobehavioral responses, dissociation

The pernicious effects of psychological trauma on the minds, bodies, and general well-being of children, adults, couples, and families are well documented (Figley & McCubbin, 1983; Follette, Ruzek, & Abueg, 1998; Green et al., 2000; Matsakis, 1994, 1996; Parson, 1994a, 1995a, 1997a, 1997b). Trauma is a physical disruption that creates discontinuities between the mind and body, between the psychological and the social, and between the past and the present. From a subjective perspective, trauma is "the experience of dread, an extreme form of fear that is induced by terror and horror . . . psychic dangers ranging from a common feared identification to states of disconnection, desolation, ego dissolution, and nonexistence" (Koch, 2000, p. 289). How severe the trauma is subjectively experienced and the meaning the victim/survivor gives the event, determine the nature and course of traumatic pathology–changes in consciousness, fear, and sense of vulnerability in one's intimate and relational world.

Multiply traumatized couples also experience interpersonal inconsistencies, disconnections, and discontinuities in self and in relating to intimate others. Multiple traumatized suffer varying degrees of derealization, depersonalization, distortion of time, and alterations in cognition, memory, somatic experience, and identity. These symptoms interfere markedly with the couple's capacity to maintain tranquility, harmony, and control in their relational lives. Trauma in both partners forms a *trauma contagion* characterized by *transactional victimizing*–an "intertraumatic" bipersonal process.

Through the intense relational transactions over time these trauma effects are structuralized into family and couple systems. Trauma-induced dissociation or post-traumatic stress disorder (PTSD) in even *one* family member may induce or exacerbate a dysfunctional couple or family system, as well as produce stress-related reactions in nondysfunctional family members (Figley, 1994; Kirschner & Kirschner, 1993; Meichenbaum, 1994). When *two* family members suffer the effects of trauma in their married life, there can be significant relational problems. Trauma-in-both create synergistic effects that are associated with a persistent trauma-destabilizing system. The couple experiences states of confusion and disorganization. These shared difficulties construct a set of *dissociative relational dynamics* that are unique for the particular couple.

In a most significant contribution, Matsakis (1994) advanced the core clinical issues pertaining to multitrauma couples, and asks a critical question bearing on the assessment and treatment of complex couple dynamics: "What happens when one trauma survivor marries another trauma survivor or when one of the partners is a dual trauma survivor?" (p. 78).

The objective of this article is to highlight and describe patterns of transactions that are unique to multitrauma couples. These are couples in which each member was exposed to one or more traumatic events, and experience the relationally-subverting symptoms of PTSD, and dissociation, and related cognitive-splitting, poor attention, and memory (DePrince & Freyd, 1999; Parson, 1994a). Also, the article presents and discusses such key concepts and issues as biopsychobehavioral trauma, responses, dissociation, attachment disturbance, assessment, and the role of therapist's functions and personality.

A treatment model is also described in which a case study is presented and treatment techniques are integratively woven into a tapestry of diverse theoretical formulations from cognitive, behavioral, to systems and psychodynamic theoretical tributaries. The treatment model described is designed for these multiply traumatized couples to facilitate integration of fragmented cognitive, affective, and behavioral elements intrapsychically and transactionally. When the treatment formally comes to an end, a new therapeutic beginning emerges: A post-treatment life plan to maintain acquired gains which serves prevention ends.

Relationship in the context of psychological trauma poses an extraordinarily difficult challenge for developing and maintaining security-engendering intimacy (Lambourn-Kavcic & Day, 1995; Matsakis, 1989a, 1989b, 2000; Spasojevic, Heffer, & Snyder, 2000). This is in part because trauma instigates intense fears in the couple-system, and exacerbates insecurities, sustains immaturities, and deepens vulnerabilities.

Empirical studies have shown that trauma-related dissociation (as opposed to dissociation caused by brain disorder or temporal lobe lesion) is associated with a variety of negative outcomes in victims of childhood sexual/physical trauma (Sanders & Giola, 1991; Saxe et al., 1993; Kimmerling, Clum, & Wolfe, 2000), in sexual assault victims (Dancu, Riggs, Hearst-Ikeda, Shoyer, & Foa, 1996), in victims/survivors of war trauma (Marmar et al., 1994), and in survivors of disasters (Brende, 1998; Cardeña & Spiegel, 1993; Parson, 1995b, 1995c).

Many dissociation-mediated outcomes have been reported in the trauma/dissociation literature. For example, studies have found a relationship between dissociation and teen-age pregnancy, poor academic performance, and repeat victimization (referred to by Kluft [1990] as the "sitting duck phenomenon"). This concept has relevance for the study and treatment of multiply traumatized couples, since it refers to *unconscious programming for repetition* of traumatic experience in human relationships. Additionally, trauma couples with dissociative illnesses show a *learned* in*ability* to use interpersonal and intrapsychic cues as signals to detour around, and to prevent internal and external "dangers" from shattering the marital relational moments. Perhaps this inability to learn from past negative experience (and so prevent future reoccurrence of trauma) may be associated with the higher probability of being unable to avert personal and interpersonal disasters.

There are several contributions in the literature on the adverse effects of traumatic dissociative symptomatology on a spouse or other family member when a loved one suffers traumatic stress symptoms. However, with the exception of Matsakis's (1989a, 1989b, 1994) contributions, there is a conspicuous absence of conceptual and therapeutic formulations on the symptomatic, characterological, and transactional problems in multiply traumatized couples.

What this article purports to add to extant literature is a new way of conceptualizing the clinical problems of multiply traumatized couples, and the evolvement of a systematic treatment model that is developmental, multitheoretical, and multiphasic. To date there are no contributions with this comprehensive, developmental and integrative perspective. Organizationally, this article begins with definitions and description of the proposed treatment approach and its rationale, as well as concepts and processes deemed integral to understanding the treatment of traumatized couples.

INTERTRAUMA COUPLES THERAPY: TREATING BIOLOGICAL, PSYCHOLOGICAL, AND RELATIONAL BARRIERS TO LOVE, INTIMACY AND FULFILLMENT

Treating dual trauma couples represent a "special circumstance" which "complicates couple therapy" in general (Compton & Follette, 1998, p. 321). Since the husband-wife pair in intertrauma treatment is seen as two *trauma-shocked* entities, each entity *constructs* and projects into his or her partner intense needs for safety, love, security, self-esteem regulation, and control. This seemingly intractable system requires a focus *on* change. Like most contemporary theories and practices of psychotherapy, the general objective of InCTC is change. But how does change occur? In trauma treatment of couples, the couple goes through a number of change stages. They begin with first, experiencing *traumatic distress* for which they seek professional assistance; second, they engage in an honest *examination* of the hard issues in the marriage, the problems, solutions, and the possibilities; third, the couple demonstrates *motivation* to face the problems, gain hope, and do the hard work needed for transformation; fourth, *acquisition* of positive, salutary gains; and fifth, the couple keeps busy in *maintenance and practice* to ensure the progress gained remains and gets better with built-in power against slipping back and decline in the relationship. Marital relationship is defined as patterned sequences of repetitive emotional and behavioral transactions between partners that control and shape intimacy, distance, sexual desire, giving, getting, and power.

Couples with a collective personal history of *multiple* traumatic events, may require an integrative model to adequately meet the broad spectrum of problems they present. This proposed model is referred to as the *intertrauma couples therapy* (InTCT). This approach is geared to meet the dual-trauma couple's self and relational needs in a systematic manner, offering the troubled couple an opportunity for change. The InTCT approach is designed for trauma victim couples in which each partner either together or separately were traumatized by the same or a different kind of trauma (i.e., war, rape, criminal assault, incest, community violence, etc.). The InTCT consists of five phases (to be described in a later portion of the article). Before proceeding with a description of shared pathology in traumatized couples, and proposed treatment process, just a word about the definition of the terms, "intertraumatic" and "dissociative attachment." In Greek the word "trauma" (a noun) means "wound," while "traumatic" (adjective) means *causing wound.* "Inter" means "mutual." *Intertraumatic* thus refers to a *reciprocal wound-generating process* in which each dyadic partner actively opens and re-opens the other's psychological wounds by persistently triggering dissociative, traumagenic defenses as an ongoing aspect of their lives together. "Dissociative attachment" refers to the state of *discontinuity of memory and identity* in the context separation anxiety-driven relational experience of a marital pair in chronic traumatic distress.

Intertrauma couple therapy aims not only to remove the walls that separate partners, but to create a bridge to connection and intimacy by assessing the self-system (intrapsychic) and the dyadic-system (transactional), and employing treatment strategies to manage trauma memories, decondition negative affects, and improve relational problems in a systematic manner. Specifically, InTCT facilitates and encourages self-system explorations and conjoint system transactions, education, affects expression, symptom management, coping augmentation, reversing cognitive distortion, while enhancing self-identity, and marital relational development.

Essentially, the InTCT model uses multiple theories of therapy integrated into a coherent system for the couple. Additionally, the model's multiple phases are each geared to address specific developmental challenges or goals. The phases involve a trauma-specific assessment process, and the management of trauma memories, dissociative symptoms, and dysfunctional relational patterns. These phases demarcate the developmental aspects of the treatment (that is, from the early state of internal and relational disorganization and impoverished coping resources to mature self functioning and enhanced relational control).

Essentially, the InTCT model derives from (1) a long trauma treatment tradition of a structured multiphase approach with multitheoretical perspective (Brown, Scheflin, & Hammond, 1998; Janet, 1904; Parson, 1984, 1999), (2) the integration of relevant trauma and relational literature, and (3) this author's experience in the treatment of multitrauma persons for over 20 years (Brown, Scheflin, & Brown, 1998; Parson, 1984, 1996a, 1998a, 1998b, 1999). Integral to the application of InTCT is an understanding of the nature of psychological trauma and associated memory disturbance, dissociative relational dynamics to include trauma-based projective identification, and biopsychobehavioral trauma responses in traumatized couples.

LEARNING AND PSYCHODYNAMIC THEORIES: TRAUMA, CONDITIONING, AND DEFENSE

Trauma theoreticians, practitioners, and research scientists have employed classical and operant learning models, biological, and psychodynamic clinical perspectives as conceptual bases to understand and treat trauma (Anderson, 1995; Brown, Scheflin, & Hammond, 1998; Coleman, Fanelli, & Gedeon, 2000; Follette, Ruzek, & Abueg, 1998; Marks & Dar, 2000; Parson, 1998a, 1998b, 1998c, 1999). Theoreticians and research scientists have used Mowrer's two factor theory to explain the development of traumatic stress disorders in war traumatic stress and rape victims (e.g., Follette, Ruzek, & Abueg, 1998; Keane, Zimmering, & Caddell, 1985; Kilpatrick et al., 1979). Classical conditioning explains fear acquisition, and operant conditioning explains the maintenance of avoidance that permeate the life of the multitrauma couple. Psychodynamic techniques seek to restructure emotions to inform cognition and relational processing.

SYSTEMS THEORY AND PARTNERS' TRAUMA-ASSOCIATED TRANSACTIONS

Systems theory is based on the premise that couples have superordinate properties beyond each other's individual psychologies, that the husband-wife system is greater than the sum of its member parts. As a systems-plus model, InTCT focuses on both the metaprocesses of couple interaction *and* each member's dissociative trauma dynamics. Systems theory espouse the view that individual and dyadic psychopathology originate in discordant interactions with parental figures. The problems presented in therapy by the multitrauma couple may or may not be influenced by parental figures, but are always dominated by each partner's internalizations of people or organizations (to whom human attributes are imputed in terms of responsibility and culpability). These internalizations are primarily unconscious programs deriving from the traumatic experience.

In line with systems approach to conceptualizing trauma-troubled relationships, the trauma-dysfunctional couple represents an active, transactional unit, which allocates to each other roles and functions shaped by the trauma. These role allocations, however, are restrictive and coercive. They limit mutual access to true feelings, and undermine flexibility and adaptability, and use of reality-oriented solutions rather than dissociative/disintegrative ones in times of crisis. In intertraumatic dynamics, both members of the dyadic pair are *projectors,* whose projections connect, intersect, and interact to create transactional structures that *contain* anxiety, rage, and dysphoric affects. Both suffer intense anxiety associated with their own traumatic tragedy.

What is projected in this bidirectional projection system are the contents of *trauma mental representations,* structures of the mind which hold vital information about the self and its relationship with others *during* and *after* the traumatic experience. These representations are internal working models that regulate and organize cognition, autobiographical memory (memory for information about the self's direct experiences), and narrative traumatic memory. Narrative traumatic memory is the recall system shaped directly by the traumatic experience: It is the autobiographical memory system altered to accommodate the new, distressing trauma information. This memory system is a post-trauma brain limbic system effect that results in fragmented, unstable, highly unpredictable memory traces. These traces are marked by persistent vividness organized around impulsive dissociative actions, images, and a disturbance of the sensorium to affect kinesthetic, proprioceptive, and temperature sensations, and the distortions of time, and space. This highly precarious system is what is projected with inconstant affect expression in which fear, chronic anxieties, narcissistic injury-based rage, and death anxiety become a central aspect of the couple's transactional system.

"What was the nature of the *new* learning that took place at the very moment of the trauma and immediately after?" This question thus is an important focus for assessment. Since representations contain the victim's experience with the perpetrator (replete with sensations, impulse, and action), or with individuals and institutions that abandon, neglect, and fail to protect.

At the time of the rape assault, Eva internalized the action, attitude, and emotions associated with the perpetrator's crime against her, as well as the specific environmental features–confused sights, sounds, kinesthetic, perceptual, and other sensory experience connected to the traumatic episode. While Eva experienced the meaning of brutal power vs. victimization, Sam viewed his company as neglectful and culpable for the blast and fire that so profoundly altered his life. Though on the surface it seemed he was bitter with a company (as opposed to a person), in effect, his sense of bitterness and entitlement was generalized to his wife and world of people.

The couple's projection-based mutuality–in adaptation and role assignment–is motivated to control the chaotic, contradictory, dissociative elements of the relationship to achieve some sense of safety and mastery. But this safety and mastery are incomplete and unreliable due to neurobiological abnormalities and instability of the trauma narrative memory system. Freud was fascinated by the ability of "perceptual reoccurrence of the same thing" to recreate inner trauma relationships that tend to dominate intrapsychic and interpersonal experience.

These pervasive trauma pathological symptoms, as mentioned before, calls for a model that employs techniques from a variety of schools of therapy integratively organized to benefit the couple. The InTCT model also thus brings together a treatment approach which uses traditional psychodynamic techniques, as well as behavioral and cognitive approaches. The system is created to increase insight and control over the intrinsic blind spots in spousal denial, defensiveness, and dissociative interactional patterns.

The InTCT treatment model represents an integration of treatment in which *individual* and *conjoint* approaches are combined to ensure that each member's self-system (intrapsychic) interacts in a dyadic-system (interpersonal/interactive) to generate the greatest and most desired treatment outcomes.

MULTITRAUMA COUPLE CASE STUDY

Eva, 41, and Samuel, 50, are a middle-class couple who are both professionals in a 10-year marriage with two children. Eva is an accountant with 11 years experience; Sam is a contractor in commercial construction with 10 years on the job. The couple were referred for marital therapy after treatment of several months for sexual dysfunction that, according to Eva, "went nowhere." Both partners complained that the other has *never* had interest in sex, each felt the other should do something about it, and both accused the other of failing to resolve their sexual problems.

Isolating themselves from each other for hours at a time on the computer, both accused the other of being a "computer junky" and "computer addict." Basically, both blamed the other for the marital conflicts and problems that threaten to destroy their marriage. Both knew the marriage was in trouble, heading for demise in divorce. Sam also blamed Eva for being insensitive to his history of trauma and his struggle to regain equilibrium. Eva expressed a similar sentiment about her husband, and neither saw the other as supportive.

Eva is a victim of a violent rape assault 10 years ago in a parking garage. This is her first marriage. Samuel is a victim of a traumatizing chemical explosion on a construction site 17 years ago that resulted in 85% of his body being severely burned. He had sustained severe bodily injuries, and endured excruciating physical pain, and disability, accompanied by persistent anxiety and depression. Eva and Sam were treated for substance abuse disorders on several occasions, each began their abuse after their respective traumatic event. Both were also treated for major depression, but neither had been assessed or treated for post-traumatic responses and PTSD.

During the initial session, both seemed very angry and disappointed at the other's inability to meet expectations, and each expressed belligerence and a demanding attitude toward the therapist. This was Sam's third marriage; the first two marriages were of short duration, and deteriorated as a direct consequence of Sam's negative trauma mood disorder, PTSD symptoms, reactive rage, sense of entitlement, and employment problems. During the initial session, Sam and Eva were wary and distrusting of the other, giving the impression of profound interpersonal turmoil and deep antipathy and couple disturbance. The mutually expressed aggression made demise of the marriage seem inevitable.

After a complete assessment of the couple, the current therapist realized that each member of the couple had a history of trauma which required a trained professional experienced in treating couples with psychological trauma. While Eva described her husband as "cold, distant, and disinterested in sex," Sam described his wife as "too aggressive, too confrontational, and too critical, moody, and demanding." Eva and Samuel had a history of problematic relationships with intimates, children, siblings, parents, and friends, as well as in the workplace, and in the community.

Eva and Sam were unable to maintain employment for long periods of time, so there were financial problems in the marriage as well. Eva's employment problems were noted in her economic descent from an accountant to becoming a substance abuse technician. Sam's descent from a contractor to a carpenter's helper was a tremendous blow to his masculine pride and "evidence" that he was no longer a competent human being. As mentioned above, both partners spent several continuous hours a day at the computer–out in cyber space. Each believed this "cyber addiction" behavior (Griffith, 1997; Huang & Alessi, 1997; Shaffer, Hall, & Bilt, 2000) was motivated to frustrate, punish, and withhold contact, love, and commitment from the other.

PRAGMATIC TECHNICAL INTEGRATION

The wide-ranging impairments seen in this multitrauma couple required pragmatic integration of disparate techniques and theories of therapy. Psychotherapy integration is gaining increasing recognition by mental health theorists, research scientists, and practitioners (Marmar et al., 1994; Norcross & Goldfried, 1992; Parson, 1984, 1995a, 1995b, 1998a, 1998b; Proshaska & Clement, 1982; Segal & Blatt, 1993; Stricker & Gold, 1993). The need for technical integration has even greater relevance in cases of multitrauma couples who endure pervasive traumatic disturbances in consciousness, memory, and physiology, as well as in intimate and social functioning (Parson, 1994a, 1996a). Elsewhere called the *intertheoretical diversiform* approach, and the *post-traumatic child therapy* model (Parson, 1984, 1994b, 1988), clinical integration is comprised of a functional admixture of behavioral, cognitive, and psychodynamic procedures, which, according to Gold (1993) and Wachtel (Wachtel & Wachtel, 1986) is based largely on empirical grounds. InTCT theory also incorporates the cognitive-dynamic information processing theory of traumatic stress syndromes (Horowitz, 1986).

From the technical point of view, behavioral procedures were used with Eva and Sam to ameliorate their symptomatic and maladaptive patterns of behaviors in the form of avoidance, intrusive ideation, aggressive outbursts, and hostile behavior toward each other. Cognitive techniques were employed to expose and modify the couple's pathogenic beliefs (or automatic thoughts), while through use of dynamic approaches the central emotional issues, fantasies, conflicts, and motives were identified and transference and countertransference manifestations explored, confronted and interpreted.

Specifically, phases 1 and 2 of the treatment aims to slow down or reverse the couple's post-traumatic declivity in mental and interpersonal functioning. This writer has found that, because of the complexities of chronic trauma symptomatology, a case management skills-oriented interventions informed by trauma theory was essential for Eva and Sam.

Intertrauma couple therapy is distinguished from nontrauma couple therapies by its diligent management of dissociation, and the neurobehavioral tendency of the mind to compulsively revisit the images, memories, thoughts, emotions, places, and people painfully associated with the original trauma (Freud, 1920; Parson, 1999). Traumatic events are experienced as assaults against the self which "set in motion archaic pathologic attempts to master what could not be mastered in the usual way" (Furst, 1967, p. 20).

The conceptual and practical underpinnings of the model highlight the clinical observation that treatment techniques that are useful at one phase of couple treatment may prove less effective at other phases. These phases of intertrauma couple therapy integrate a number of learning and cognitive conceptual streams in contemporary treatment: cognitive content-oriented approach (the identification of negative beliefs or "self talk"), the semantic network model of internal memory structure to traumatization (development of "fear structures" in memory), and personal account/narratives (Foa & Rothbaum, 1998; Follette, Ruzek, & Abueg, 1998; Marks & Dar, 2000; Meichenbaum, 1994; Parson, 1997a, 1998a, 1998b). As a multiple theoretical perspective therapy, intertrauma couple treatment also incorporates psychodynamic techniques, which promote biopsychobehavioral integration of relational and attachment factors (Parson, 1984, 1988, 1998a, 1998b).

Deriving generally from the trauma paradigm and treatment tradition (Brown, Scheflin, & Hammond, 1998; Janet, 1904; Parson, 1984, 1998a, 1998b, 1999; Ulman & Brothers, 1989), the phases of InTCT are: (1) *Assessment and Orientation to Intertrauma Therapy,* (2) *Stabilization and Counter-Reactivity Relational Training,* (3) *Individualized Trauma Explorations and Neurocognitive Processing,* (4) *Conjoint Emotional Processing and Relational Integration,* and (5) *Post-Integration Life Skills Practice.*

PHASE 1.
ASSESSMENT AND ORIENTATION
TO INTERTRAUMA THERAPY

Assessment in intertrauma treatment is a vital activity, because it is important to understand the contributions of each partner to the couple-system. Generally, assessment contributes important information on the relative weights of childhood developmental history and trauma-based influences on the couple's presenting trauma cognitions, primitive fears, insecurities, and fundamental immaturities in personality functioning before and after the trauma. Ultimately, assessment ascertains to a clinical and experiential path from transactional fury to breaking through barriers to love (Bergner, 2000).

Recognizing and Assessing Biopsychobehavioral Responses in Multitrauma Couples

PTSD and dissociation represent biopsychobehavioral syndromes, reflecting alterations in the victim's biology, psychology, and social/behavioral systems in the aftermath of violent human and natural catastrophic events such as war, rape, torture, terrorism, and disasters (Arata et al., 2000; Brende, 1998; Parson, 1995a, 1995b). These reactions and disorders also come from exposure to such events as the Oklahoma bombing, and the shootings at Columbine High School in Colorado, the Jewish Community Center in southern California, and the shooting in a church in Fort Worth, Texas in recent months. Violence has always left its indelible trauma imprint upon the minds and bodies of innocent victims, but also of culpable perpetrators of violence in East Timor, Kosovo, Rwanda, India, and Pakistan, Chechnya, Angola, Nigeria, and Colombia. Trauma produces disturbances in "arousal, behavior, cognition, and physiological functioning and most body systems . . . affect[ing] reproductive growth, thyroid, and immune functions" (Schwartz & Kowalski, 1993, p. 285). Since biopsy-chobehavioral trauma responses in couples are chiefly "hard-wired" into the central nervous system effecting an emotional conditional response (Kolb, 1987, 1993), only a multifaceted approach to treat-ment that employs cognitive, behavioral/learning, and psychodynamic approaches to treatment can realistically meet the couple's needs (Brown, Scheflin, & Hammond, 1998; Everly, 1993; Follette, Ruzek, & Abueg, 1998; Marks & Dar, 2000; Marmar et al., 1994a; Parson, 1984, 1999).

Biological Responses:
Neurological Impediment to Relational Harmony

Highlighting the biological roots of PTSD, Kolb (1987, 1993) theo-rized that the major symptoms of PTSD were a result of an emotional conditioned response. The disorder develops from the subjective ap-praisal of *mortal threat,* and subsequent reexperiencing of fear and terror. Kolb maintains that in PTSD there is repetitive high-intensity emotional signals within the central nervous system, which may lead eventually to neural change, neural damage, or, in very severe chronic cases, even to cell death. This change, in turn, may lead to hypersensi-tivity and accompanying *impairment in normal habituation and learn-ing.* These impairments have serious relational consequences for the couple. Among these are dissociative relational transactions, attach-ment disturbance, disturbed body systems, affective stress response, dissociation and diminished ability to learn (and are explored during assessment process), and multiplicity of post-traumatic fears. The cog-nitive stress response, and the behavioral stress symptoms are also accompaniments of traumatic stress, and require assessment as well (Parson, 1994a, 1994b, 1998a, 1998b).

Dissociative relational transactions. Though not well understood dissociation is believed to play a major role in post-traumatic interper-sonal responses (Brown, Scheflin, & Hammond, 1998; Parson, 1994a, 1994b).

The assessment of dissociative symptoms is an important aspect of the overall assessment/diagnostic process (Carlson, 1997; Dutton, 1998; Marmar et al., 1994b, Foy & Parson, 1997a, 1997b, 1998a, 1998b). Dissociation is a central response in psychological trauma, and, therefore, cannot be ignored in couple assessment process. Ordi-narily, the individual's memory is *associated.* Dissociation is the opposite of *association*–or biopsychological connectivity between and among the functions of the self like memory, affect, and behavior. Dissociation represents a *discontinuity* of consciousness (Spiegel, 1991) with periodic subjective experience of *being-in-pieces*. Discontinuity of consciousness is observed in the various relationship-subverting forms of dissociation; namely, depersonalization, amnesia, fugue, and dissociative identity disorder (APA, 1994).

Couples with dissociative attachment experience the opposite of *associative attachment,* or the integrative, trusting and calmative connectedness that promotes healthy adaptation for the couple. Dissociative attachment represents a biopsychobehavioral dyssynchrony in human relating, with amnesic and depersonalization aspects. This form of disturbed relating is hypersensitive to criticism to narcissistic insults which result in narcissistic rage, generalized defensiveness, and vulnerability to emotional hyperreactivity due to deficiency in anxiety management. For this couple life often appears as a life-and-death search for *safe anchoring* in any animate, or even inanimate structure, or experience (as in altered consciousness caused by drug abuse, hypersex, workaholism, etc.).

Dissociation, according to the DSM-IV, "is a disruption in the usually integrated functions of consciousness, memory, identity, or perception of the environment" (APA, 1994, p. 477). When husband *and* wife both experience this trauma-born "disruption in the usual integrated functions," the ordinary challenges of living, loving, and growing toward each other over time are seriously compromised. There are two kinds of dissociation–normal and pathological. Dissociative responses are a common part of our daily existence. What is being discussed here in traumatized couples is pathological dissociation. "Pathological dissociation . . . [involves] a damaged . . . identity that distorts the victim's self-image, relational functioning, and representational memory system" (Parson, 1999, p. 20).

In terms of defense organization, pathological dissociation turns off the switch of awareness to forestall future threats of imminent mishap and violence, and the reexperiencing of disorganization, and death anxiety. Dissociation is related to somatic forms of trauma memory processing, which, when compared with psychological processing, is less efficient and reliable. Thus, somatic functioning in couple-relating may be particularly enigmatic because it is relatively ineffectual in integrating identity, thought, affect, memory, perception, and sensation and behavior (Parson, 1984).

It represents a *failure in adaptive, integrative neurocognitive regulation*. Each member of the couple is thus "governed" by persistent threats of dissociative reliving and breakdown (Parson, 1984, 1994a, 1994b, 1996a, 1996b, 1996c) in their daily life together. This kind of reliving and anticipated catastrophe is subjectively felt as threats of the emergence of dissociated terror, and feelings of annihilation, separation anxiety, undergirded by neurobiological arousal. Hyer et al. (1993) concur that dissociation is related to "excessive fearfulness, symptoms of strange experiences, and high tonic psychophysiological states" (Hyer et al., 1993, p. 519).

Over the past two decades, there has been a resurgence of interest in dissociative disorders. This is due in part to the increase in war trauma and sexual abuse studies. In traumatherapy with couples each member of the dyadic pair has had a personal history of exposure to one or more traumatic events (e.g., child sexual abuse, sexual assault, war-zone violence, community violence, traumatic burns, etc.).

Janet (1907) believed that dissociation was probably an integral aspect of all mental disorders. While it was Paul Briquet (Gil, 1991), the French psychiatrist who first formulated the concept of dissociation, it was Pierre Janet who introduced a coherent theory in 1889. He found dissociation to be implicated in all forms of trauma and abuse, and maintained that it may play a role in the creation of all neurotic disturbances, fugue states, psychogenic amnesia and multiple personality. Memory was seen as the core organizing apparatus of the mind in that it was intrinsic to the continuity of consciousness, the disturbances of which were seen in conditions as trauma-specific hyperamnesias and amnesias.

Dissociation, therefore, represents self and relational impairments that need to be assessed and understood. Treatment is then geared to reverse these negative relational processes and move the couple forward to coherence, control, and intimacy.

Trauma and attachment disturbance. Human attachment is a primary biological force in people's lives. While positive attachment facilitates heightened self-esteem, and the building of trust and empathy for others, traumatic attachment is defensive and blindly passionate, featuring an identity system that is vulnerable to disintegrative anxiety, and the need to merge with another person for psychological survival. After experiencing a traumatic event, most people find solace, comfort, and support from others, which is experienced as salutary and very beneficial (Collins & Feeney, 2000; Pierce, Sarason, & Sarason, 1996).

For the multitrauma couple, the sense of internal and interpersonal security and connection are damaged, resulting in disturbances in attachment. In traumatic stress, moreover, with its characteristic emotional conditioning response, the individual's sense of well-being and neuropsychological integrity are continually threatened by disquieting bio-alarm systems that activate arousal, and spark anxiety, fear, and terror.

Trauma shatters human attachment by disrupting the psychobiology of the self that governs the integration of conscious thought, emotion, and behavior. This shattering of the self's biological integrity adversely affect adaptive connectivity of self to others and of others to self. According to Bowlby, intimate relationships consist of the attachment system and the caregiving system (Collins & Feeney, 2000; Parson, 1994b, 1995a). Emotional connection between persons is so important for human life, growth, survival, and adaptation, that, developmentally, this connection in early life is not left to chance alone: The relationship is partly neurophysiologically wired.

The neurobiology for human bonding involves brain amines in the developing brain (Kraemer, 1992) that is influenced by emotional and behavioral aspects of a relationship, such as rituals like cooing, mutual timing, signaling, smiling, cognitions, feelings, and demonstrations of respect (Field, 1985; Parson, 1998a, 1999). There is a biological basis for healthy, integrative human relating, and, as Jeremy Holmes holds, there is also a "biological basis for psychotherapy" (Holmes, 1993, p. 430). This "neurological bridging" facilitates a neurobiological synchrony for successful relational bonding. Positive attachment also promotes empathy, sense of security, hope, positive expectations for self, others, and the future, and the social connection that undergird survival, adaptation, and coping.

Body systems and post-traumatic effects. Trauma affects body systems involving reproductive growth, thyroid functions, and immune operations (Schwartz & Kowalski, 1993). Some responses seen in couples include gastrointestinal disturbances, stomachaches, headaches, sweating, increased heart rate, and jitteriness. Due to the mind/body connection between trauma and physical health, partners often present significant medical problems (Schnurr & Spiro, 1999; Turkus, 1998; Wagner et al., 2000).

Affective traumatic stress response. The multiple-trauma couple respond with mood disorders and a variety of emotional responses to a number of losses–vanishing of innocence, inestimable loss of supportive and gratifying relationships, and the perceived self-failure to control or modulation turbulent emotions that interfere with marital harmony.

Dysphoric stress response. Traumatized couples often experience profound levels of depression, grief, sadness, guilt, shame, separation anxiety, rage, and other dysphoric feelings as a response to pervasive disruptions, and helplessness and hopelessness in their lives. The traumatic rupturing of previously established attachment may be a source of dysphoric mood and anguish for the couple, especially for Eva. These negative affects result in reduction of gratifying activities, insensate sexual desire, fear of intimacy, marital isolation and discord, and boundary and management problems.

Depression is a frequent comorbid condition that accompanies PTSD in multiple-trauma couples. With Eva and Sam, the affective problem of learned helplessness was reflected in the feeling that their relationship problems would never improve, that the nightmares both suffered would never be relieved. Their sense of helplessness, emotional heaviness and gloom were pervasive in their daily lives. This state of dysphoria was undergirded by anhedonia, emotional rigidity, constriction of affect, and a trigger-ready tendency to relational reactivity and hostility.

Low affect tolerance. The effects of overwhelming events may be called a neurobiological "meltdown," that supersensitizes the victim to the ubiquitous perception of threatening signals. This hypersensitivity is accompanied by strong emotional reactivity, numbing and avoidance, and an ineffectual coping capacity in modulating anxiety and aggression, due in part to brain changes in neurotransmitter systems. These changes leave the partners with a subjective feeling of being defenseless, and being totally at the whims of wildly regulated emotions, a sense of confusion, irritability, amnesia, sleep disturbance, depersonalization, and a basic loss of capacity to understand symbolic expressions and use symbols. Modulating strong affects is a significant problem for traumatized individuals and couples, the consequences of which is explosive emotional reactivity. These problems are far-reaching for healthy couple functioning. Low affect tolerance is an important consideration in intertrauma assessment and treatment.

Post-traumatic fears. The multitrauma couple system is fraught with a multiplicity of fears that impact the relationship. These are addressed in various phases of couple traumatherapy. The emergent fears from metaperceptions of trauma-based cues are referred to as the five post-traumatic fears:

Fear of revictimization. This post-traumatic response manifests in the couple's tendency to see the other as potential victimizer or betrayer, originating primarily in the traumatic experience.

Fear of future somatopsychic reenactments. Many trauma victims experience somatic equivalents of anxiety, which induces feelings of vulnerability, and the undermining of self control. Somatic reliving by partners create mutual irritability, impatience, desire to retreat in anxious isolation. Assessing sexual, somatic and medical complaints are an important aspect of Phase 1 clinical activities.

Fear of intimacy, engulfment, and being controlled. For the multitrauma couple, these post-traumatic reactions derive from the couple's view of closeness as a threat to a fragile identity, and a tenuously-organized self-esteem. Matsakis's (2000) concept of "emotional claustrophobia" is relevant here. It is the persistent fear of feeling engulfed, suffocated, and trapped in human relationships.

Fear over eruption of violent, destructive impulses. Due to disordered neurobiological processes, cognitive distortions, and poor boundary definition in trauma couples, each member fears acting on violent impulses toward each other, or toward others.

Fear of punishment, and being judged and humiliated. Self-blame and personalized responsibilitizing guilt are common problems among traumatized individuals and couples. Fear of being judged, condemned, and humiliated are often enacted in the couple's relating.

PTSD. Assessment of PTSD is an important aspect of the assessment process. This disorder occurs when a person is exposed to an overwhelming event, and then experiences three kinds of symptoms: reliving, avoidance, and arousal (APA, 1994). These responses and related research have led many observers to view PTSD as a biological disorder (Parson, 1984; van der Kolk, 1984; van der Kolk, 1996; van der Kolk, McFarlane, & Weisaeth, 1996). Though these responses may lay dormant during a latency period, the trauma victim may experience psychological distress and/or physiological arousal when exposed to events that symbolize or resemble the original event. The implications of these symptoms and reactions for the couple system are very significant.

Symbolizing trauma elements. Multitrauma couples like Eva and Sam often encounter many personal, sensory, temporal, and environmental stimuli which "remind" them of their original trauma. Anniversary dates and stimuli associated with that date trigger reliving experiences that often interfere with the relationship. There were times, according to Eva, that Sam's behavior induced feelings of fear and anticipated attack–reminiscent of the sexual assault.

Persistent avoidance and loss of interest. These symptoms were noted in Eva and Sam's life together. Their overuse of the computer referred to by them as "computer addiction" is one manifestation of these relational problems. Numbing and avoidance symptoms often prove to be *controls that are out of control*: They subvert intimacy and communication in the couple's life. When memories of the trauma are triggered, symptoms of arousal, anxiety, and fear are here persistently avoided in thought, behavior, and biology.

Irritability. Irritability reflects the neurobiological abnormalities which are empirically associated with PTSD and dissociation. Sam and Eva showed signs of being "edgy" with one another. Each accused the other of "going off" in anger.

Sleep disturbance. With Eva and Sam there were persistent symptoms of hyperarousal with accompanying difficulties falling or remaining asleep. Lack of re-generating sleep was another source of irritability, impatience, and trigger-ready explosive anger.

Hypervigilance. This symptom in the lives of Sam and Eva was presented repeatedly during the assessment and treatment processes. Hypervigilance is a state of paranoidal hyperarousal in which partners anticipate "attack" from the spouse and so braces emotionally to defend against the attack and forestall future attacks by exaggerated "overkill" responses.

Exaggerated startle reactions. This symptom was seen in the couple, when a partner would drop a pot or pan in the kitchen, approached suddenly from behind, or yelled. Startle reactions are subjectively experienced by the couple as a loss of control and regulation, and are often accompanied by heightened anxiety, shame, and embarrassment.

Outbursts of anger. Both partners of the couple complained about the other's outbursts of anger and hostility. Partners are often frightened by their own and partner's anger and rage reactions, because these emotions are experienced as very threatening to the relationship in that they trigger memories of loss of control, helplessness, violence, and death anxiety.

Psychotherapy for PTSD. Medications are an important adjunct to intertrauma couple therapy. Psychopharmacologic agents classified as SSRIs (selective serotonin reuptake inhibitors) have been reported to be useful for a variety of PTSD symptoms–re-experiencing, avoidance, and arousal (Friedman, 2000). Trauma expert consensus has produced meaningful guidelines for trauma sufferers (Foa, Davidson, & Frances, 1999). Such as with Sam and Eva assessment revealed significant autonomic arousal, nightmares, irritability, intrusive thoughts, and sleep disturbance.

Psychological Responses

Cognitive Stress Response. Cognition in traumatic stress presents a significant problem in the life of the couple, and is manifested in partners' difficulty in the use of symbols and semantic representations, as well as in the overuse of black-white thinking. Moreover, primitive, dissociative psychological defenses tend to adversely affect adaptive thinking, reducing general cognitive efficacy in relational communication. These deficits may adversely affect the couple's ability to learn new ways of relating to each other, and meeting each other's needs. These deficits along with trauma-based reliance on somatic processes, denial, avoidance, explosive anger, withdrawal, and numbing constitute the cognitive stress response.

Trauma-Based Projective Identification. In dissociative bonding it is the couple's traumas which keep the partners "instrumentally tied" to each other through the relatively ineffectual defense strategy, *projective identification* as a maladaptive unconscious quest for a relationship. This defense was first identified by Melanie Klein, advanced in the psychodynamic literature by writers like Grotstein (1981), and applied to couples therapy by Rutan and Smith (1985). This mechanism is generally understood in psychodynamic theory as a process by which one individual attributes disowned parts of self to a target person, and, in turn, the target individual is induced to behave in ways that are consistent with the projections (or attributions).

This author prefers the term, *trauma-based projective identification* (TBPI) for intertrauma relational problems marked by feared, hated, and disowned aspects of self. In TBPI, one trauma partner ejects out of self unbearable trauma-influenced perceptions, ideas, and feelings (too debilitating to be contained within), and "translocates" them *into* the other's traumatized self-system. Through these shared "delusional cognitions" the projecting partner unconsciously manipulates to control the other who is now in a tangible, concrete, physical/psychologic representation of *internalized trauma personalities.*

This projection-altered couple system aims to control the *return of dissociated trauma self- and other-representations*; that is, the system functions to stave off gush of sudden, uncontrollable imagery, memories, and terror-based affects. Perpetrator psychology, the behavior principles that highlight the victims' *identification-with-the-perpetrator* dynamics by which they internalize attitudinal and behavioral predispositions, is also essential in the assessment of human-design trauma victims (Brown, Scheflin, & Hammond, 1998; Parson, 1984, 1998a, 1998b, 1999; Salter, 1995).

Trauma and Self-Realizing. Often clinicians become so engrossed with the dramatic symptoms of the intertrauma couple that they may lose sight of an equally important dimension of the assessment and treatment process; namely, identifying areas in which each partner improved in areas of self-realizing, insight, courage, diminished self-interest and increased concern for others' welfare, while augmenting psychological-mindness, and personal hardiness.

BEHAVIORAL RESPONSES

Dissociation involves on/off switches that cause abrupt and unpredictable behavior that makes the couple's ability to think, learn, plan, perceive clearly, and make rational choices a true challenge. Multi-trauma couples whose relational world function well possess (1) an integration of consciousness, (2) ability to remember proximal and distal aspects of mutual experience, (3) a relatively cohesive identity, and (4) reality-oriented, non-distorted perceptions. Difficulties in any of these areas result in trauma behavioral problems that may seriously hamper the couple's capacity for love and relational harmony. Thus, understanding PTSD and dissociation, and related behavioral transactions in multiply traumatized couples is essential.

Behaviorally, traumatized people are often impulse-driven in relationships, and may engage in psychological and physical self-attacks ranging from mild to severe deprecating self-statements, to wrist-cutting, and other extreme self-harming and self-mutilating behaviors. Various forms of self-abuse have been associated empirically with trauma-based dissociation (Becker-Lausen, Sanders, & Chinsky, 1995; Brodsky, Cloitre, & Dulit, 1995; Parson, 1994a, 1996b, 1996c; Zlotnick, Shea, Pearlstein, Simpson, Costello, & Begin, 1996). Self-abuse and partner-abuse may be two sides of the same coin, and so needs to be assessed as well.

Some couples' negative unconscious cognitions are geared to gain control over internalized terror, and regulate overwhelming dysphoric affectivity. Eva and Sam experienced little or no fulfillment from interacting with each other, in part because they were too preoccupied with protecting themselves against revisitations of old memories, fears, and annihilation anxiety linked to internalized trauma-based presences. Other couples may engage in physical rough play and "live on the edge" (to manage dead feelings inside), and show poor social functioning, along with addictions, perversions, and anxiety-driven compulsions.

ORGANIZATION OF ASSESSMENT PROCESS: EVALUATION, FORMULATION, TREATMENT PLAN, AND FEEDBACK

Comprehensive trauma couple assessment begins with an understanding of the pair's immediate post-traumatic complaints and symptoms, and the nature of marital interaction. The assessor looks at the couple's personality functioning *before* the traumatic event, examines responses *during* the traumatic event(s), and the specific nature of post-traumatic regression, symptoms, and disorganization *after* the event. The therapist employs direct observation, structured clinical tests, and, if necessary, administration of mental and social tests.

In this phase the couple is assessed in order to develop a clinical formulation of the problem and a plan for treatment. Intertrauma assessment involves both intrapsychic dynamics and behavioral transactions, the couple's family histories, as well as each partner's developmental, maturational, and traumatopsychic histories. The trauma treatment therapist seeks data on each spouse's family background: how each spouse's father and mother raised children, and describe each parent's style of interaction and values, as well as individual and collective family-of-origin personality styles. The assessment process has three general goals: trauma history formulation, treatment plan, and an initial positive, structured therapeutic engagement to convince the couple that therapy can work.

Certain precautions are essential considerations for getting the treatment off to a good start. Thus, the assessment begins with a conjoint interview with the couple with clearly articulated groundrules that structure the interaction between each partner and between the couple and the therapist. The therapist guards against the eruption of uncontrolled, vitriolic exchanges of insulting or narcissistic injurious charges and blaming and countercharges and counterblaming. Often if attacks are allowed to occur without a direct response from the therapist, the couple may leave the first visit demoralized, having felt attacked in the presence of another and embarrassed (the couple may thus lose confidence in the ability of the therapist and the process to keep partners safe and protect self-esteem). When partners in couple treatment feel attacked, they also feel helpless as trust degenerates into renewed bouts of fear, emotional reactivity, blaming, and general negativity.

Ostensibly, Eva and Sam came to therapy to find new strategies to improve the quality of their relationship, despite their pessimism and hopelessness. This reality proved to be of value in subsequent sessions when a partner may have lost sight of the reason for which he or she had sought treatment in the first place. Though it's unrealistic to expect all problems to be solved in the first meeting, the couple needs to experience *hope* that positive outcomes are possible in the *near* future. When the first session begins down the path of loss of emotional control, bickering, and vitriolic name-calling and blaming the partners do not have sufficient insight into their own motivations and behavior to realize that the first session's negativity will change over time. Because of this, the therapist intervenes early with a systematic structure that may be internalized by the "out of control" couple or partner.

The first order of business is to control emotional reactivity and offer a vision for possibilities, for hope that things will improve with hard work they are both capable of doing. Hope, courage, and faith are central problem areas in troubled couples' lives. Eva and Sam found emotional reactivity and hopelessness to threaten to the viability of their marriage relationship, despite their pessimism and hopelessness.

The first session is structured so that it becomes a truly *therapeutic rendezvous* (that is, a healing opportunity for two warring factions to experience brief moments of positive, integrative vistas of how life could be with professional help and relational harmony). Thus, the *first* visit is to imbue the couple with hope and positive possibilities-an outlook for commitment and positive change.

In structuring the initial session with Eva and Sam, the therapist asked each partner to describe the problems from her and then from his perspective. Each partner is given ten minutes. During this time the other partner listens *only*, restraining self from responding to what the other is saying. After Eva's ten minutes had expired, Sam gave his perspective on the problem. Eva was then allowed to react in just one ten-minute statement to Sam's statement on their relational problems, after which Sam gave his reactions to his wife's accounts. For this volatile couple, this proved to be the first therapeutic lesson in emotional non-reactivity and positive listening behavior. The session ended with a shared, preliminary formulation of the problems as understood by the therapist up to that point.

In the first session the therapist explained the goals, benefits, focus, and methods of intertrauma therapy in language which they could understand. For this couple, first-phase procedures enhanced the sense of mutual expectations between couple and therapist, and the aligning of these expectations with reality. Phase 1 offered this overwhelmed, insecure couple some reassurance that they will improve as time goes on to get positive long-term results.

The therapist informs the couple about the next assessment session, and the course of intertrauma treatment. The second first phase session is also structured: a ten-minute brief recounting by the therapist of last session's highlights of each partner's strengths and problems areas. Next, the husband is given a brief questionnaire that assesses areas of marital distress, commitment to working to improve the relationship, domestic violence, and direction and amount of desired change (Jacobson & Christensen, 1996). He sits in an adjoining office or quiet space. As he responds to the marital questionnaires, his wife is given a comprehensive interview consisting of two structured interviews: a 20-minute PTSD Symptoms Scale–Interview (PSS-I; Foa et al., 1993; Foa & Tolin, 2000), and the 15-minute Dissociative Experiences Scale (DES, Carlson & Putnam, 1993 or Steinberg, 1995). The couple meets after the assessment procedures questions are answered, and the couple is informed about the third first phase session.

At the third session the order of assessment activities are reversed: Eva is given the marital distress questionnaires, while Sam is interviewed by the therapist using traumatic stress and dissociation assessment instruments, such as the fifteen-minute Trauma Assessment for adults (TAA; Resnick, 1996) and the DES. Stressor assessment/ screening is essential in order to determine whether one or both members of the pair had experienced single or multiple traumatic episodes (Green et al., 2000). Assessment of substance as a self-medicating device was also done with this couple.

At the fourth session, the couple is given feedback on the clinician's clinical impressions and a formulation of the problem and the treatment plan. Though the previous three sessions represented the beginning of the therapeutic venture with the couple, the therapy proper begins during this phase. At this juncture in the first phase therapy process, the couple engages in a true dialogue with the therapist–asking, pondering, wondering, deciding. Eva and Sam were free to decide not to continue the treatment.

The assessment revealed that both partners had chronic PTSD and dissociative symptoms, establishing them as a multitrauma couple with a significant level of post-traumatic personality changes. Additionally, there was a high level of marital distress, moderate level of commitment to work hard and improve the relationship, and the presence of deep mutual distrust. As parents, the couple expressed their concern about their failure in this area of family life. Results also showed they were pessimistic that things would ever change, but they decided to remain in therapy. Feedback discussions and exchanges, organized within the "five-Cs framework" (Nichols, 1998), were fertile ground for learning about the details of each partner's trauma and post-trauma experiences, about the various ways one partner's trauma interacts with the other's trauma-based thinking patterns, beliefs, and general expectations of healing the marriage, as well as their commitment, caring, conflict and ability to compromise, and contracting.

The assessment also revealed a number of dynamic themes, as well as many ways each spouse had programmed the other to enact specific roles linked to dissociative aspects of their partner's personality (that are either feared, missing, unacceptable, or infantile). For Eva and Sam psychological abuse, as described by experts (Follingstad & De-Hart, 2000; Loring, 1994), was a significant manifestation of their trauma transactions. Trauma-based psychosomatic symptoms and medical complaints were found in both partners (Wijma et al., 2000). In general, it is critical that this phase does not terminate before the specific problems that brought the couple into treatment are highlighted, thoroughly explored, and the couple feels understood. In fact, the first session needs to address the couple's presenting complaints directly, ensuring the partners *know* they are understood, and that hope for a better future is warranted.

PHASE 2.
STABILIZATION, COUNTER-REACTIVITY RELATIONAL TRAINING, AND ACCEPTANCE

Stabilization is essential for integration, and the techniques of this phase continue from the last phase. The primary function is to reduce and then eliminate emotional reactivity *within* and *between* the marital partners. The basic theme of this phase in couple treatment is: "Do no harm, mental nor physical: don't react!" When either Eva or Sam was unable to contain intense negative feelings and made personal attacks, the therapist re-focused the out-of-control partner on emotional control and behavioral restraint. Reactivity undermines the ideal of stabilization, a key prerequisite for trauma integration and building a positive relationship. These goals are in part achieved through cognitive-behavioral traumatic stress management, a set of procedures geared to restructure the couple's trauma-distorted thought patterns (that instigate bio-alarm reactions, anxiety, and depression, and impulsivity) while targeting of specific problematic behaviors. The traumatic stress management techniques for this phase with Eva and Sam were: behavioral rehearsal, homework assignment, stress management/relaxation training, deconditioning of negative affects, and biofeedback for autonomic system regulation, the systematic altering of the violence- and tragedy-associated automatic assumptions (helped partners with their anger, relational narcissistic wounds, impulsivity, helplessness, depression, and avoidance), and psychopharmacology in small dosages to ameliorate intrusive thoughts, anxiety, depression, and physiological arousal, irritability, and insomnia. Psychoeducational procedures designed specifically for the intertrauma couple (or for the "PTSD couple") are an integral dimension of the therapy (Rabin & Nardi, 1991).

In this phase the couple also learns to regulate emotional reactivity by challenging and questioning automatic assumption, such as, "half of me is gone: my life is over"; "My inner torture will never go away because I am bad"; "she doesn't love me: she wishes me dead"; "Life is worthless because of the damage done to me"; "He hates me!", etc. Self-instruction is also used to assist the couple in increasing control over intrusive thoughts, fear, anger outbursts and general emotion reactivity, and anxiety. Self-instructional training (Meichenbaum, 1994) was done in three steps. First, the couple's negative thinking is explored to reduce the chances of relationship-destroying affect-reactivity and being overwhelmed; second, the couple learns how to generate incompatible thinking, facilitated by overt, positive self-statements which over time are repeated subvocally (covert). Third, the couple uses behavioral rehearsal to increase coping and mastery skills. As negative relationship-based emotions and cognitions are processed, intertrauma therapy assesses and encourages the softer emotions and the development of empathic accuracy, and cognitive perspective-taking.

PHASE 3.
INDIVIDUALIZED TRAUMA EXPLORATIONS AND NEUROCOGNITIVE PROCESSING

The neurocognitive processing of the trauma is critical for integration and attachment-building to occur. Failure in trauma cognitive-affective informational processing underlies PTSD and dissociation (Amir et al., 1998; Horowitz, 1986). This phase attempts to deal with two biopsychological dilemmas: the *dilemma of memory* (unbidden remembrance and amnesia for desired details), and the *double character of anxiety*. For on the one hand, the anxiety-laden trauma response "is often expedient and functional in the face of 'real' [traumatic] danger; and [on] the other, it can become a reaction that reproduces, as it were, the very danger it strives to react against"(Weber, 2000, p. 88).

Repairing disjointed, fear-based memory traces essentially recognizes that the trauma victim's problems represent a primary *somatic organization* rather than a *psychological organization*, the former being a relatively feeble, unintegrated system, while the latter reflects higher levels of integration and control. The intertrauma treatment techniques include trauma narrative therapy (Foa & Rothbaum, 1998; Meichenbaum, 1994), a way to transform short, simple, concrete, inarticulate trauma narratives (characteristics of somatic organization) into longer, more complex ones (characteristics of verbal/semantic representation). Also associated with somatic level of trauma processing is the memory system Bower calls "behavioral memory system," distinguished from the more advanced social autobiographical memory system (Brown, Scheflin, & Hammond, 1998).

In assessing memory systems in the trauma victim, the clinician, attending to the clinical challenges posed by the dilemma of memory and the dilemma of the trauma response begins the work of undoing the *compulsion to redo* (passionate recurring attempts to "get it right" and gain control over traumatic suffering) that alternates with a *compulsion to disavow* (in order to restore pre-trauma sense of control). In the psychoanalytic literature the compulsion to repeat traumatic distress is referred to as the "repetition compulsion," a central mechanism in the trauma response (Freud, 1920; Herman, 1992; Levy, 2000; van der Kolk, 1996).

Exposure to the feared stimuli, whether imaginal, *in vivo*, vicarious, rapid, slow, continuous, intermittent, single vs. combined techniques, is essential in any comprehensive treatment strategy for anxiety disorders (Marks & Dar, 2000; Parson, 1998a, 1998b). In intertrauma couple assessment, each partner is seen individually for several sessions, depending on the nature of the trauma and degree of subsequent spontaneous recovery to date. For Eva, her rape traumatic experience was the focus; for Sam, his burn trauma was the focus. Frederick (1985) noted that "merely talking [about the trauma] . . . will not suffice in undoing serious psychic trauma in either adults or children" (p. 92). Thus, specific direct exposure techniques were essential for this couple during this phase.

This phase is ushered in *only* when sufficient trust has been developed in the therapeutic relationship, and the couple has had relaxation training, and mastered a relaxation procedure. This may take several weeks or months. The time depends on a number of variables such as coping capacity, the nature, intensity, and duration of the initial traumatic event, the persistence of traumatic symptomatology, as well as on pre- and post-trauma personality factors, previous traumas, and available posttrauma social supports.

Imaginal re-experiencing procedures were important to emotionally go back *in vivo* to the scene–to the very place of the rape, for Eva, and to the place of the explosion and burn, for Sam. While at these sites of trauma, the partner processes the painful affects and accompanying physiological arousal through cognitive and dynamic procedures. The treatment also involved identifying and activating deeply imbedded "fear structures," then imbedding new information and affect processing to aid integration (Foa & Rothbaum, 1998; Parson, 1998a, 1998b).

After the requisite acquisition of trust, and relaxation training have been mastered by the partner, the therapist introduces the trauma scene and asks the individual partner to search his or her memory, while remaining as relaxed as possible. The therapist conducts thorough behavioral and cognitive analysis derived from data gathered during the first two phases, and the beginning of this phase. These data include the partners' trauma histories, replete with visual, auditory, tactile, and olfactory aspects, as well as the development of a traumatic imagery hierarchy, ranging from low anxiety to high anxiety cues (the therapist emphasized both stimulus that originated in the trauma and response dimensions at the time of the event), and later gradually move up the hierarchy of cues. The therapist also offered the couple useful strategies to help them maintain the gains they had achieved. Eye Movement Desensitization and Reprocessing (EMDR; Shapiro & Forrest, 1997) techniques proved to be valuable adjuncts to the treatment during this and other phases for the couple.

PHASE 4.
CONJOINT RELATIONAL/EMOTIONAL PROCESSING AND INTEGRATION

Unlike the previous phases in which behavioral and cognitive techniques were used, this phase primarily employs psychodynamic approaches. The technical strategy here is to work through trauma relational elements in the therapy. Dynamic processes were necessary with Eva and Sam because they offer language . . . the dynamic tool through which the individual negotiates meaning and transforms the nonverbal organized pattern of relatedness" (Appelman, 2000, p. 192). Dynamic relational techniques, especially transference and countertransference analyses, facilitated Eva's capacity to tolerate strong emotions, and later integrate powerful emotions associated with a violent internalized abuser representation. Feelings of fear, guilt, revulsion, depression, and rage were processed. For Sam, his deep sense of inadequacy, distrust, blaming attitude, low self-esteem, rage, depression, and profound isolation were explored and worked through using dynamic procedures. Both partners had significant borderline personality traits and avoidance, trauma-originating dependency and immaturities in self and relational functioning, as well as an absence of self-caring desire and skills, narcissistic rage over personal losses in physical health, bodily injuries and suffering, sadness, grief, and disappointment.

As treatment progressed with Eva and Sam during this phase, Eva and Sam began to experience each other in a different way. Intense relationship-subverting emotional issues were explored with a focus on rebuilding the relationship, beginning with courtship intimacy and interest, encouraging the couple to go out on dates once a week, to recapture the emotional splendor, closeness, and excitement they once had with each other.

As time progressed, the partners experienced their lives moving from trauma-fixated, immature dependency to growth-enhancing interdependence, a developmental outcome of positive treatment effects. According to Winnicott (1975), two kinds of dependencies pervade people's experience, immature dependency and mature dependency. Ordinarily, human dependency is a normal and positive lifetime need and tendency: No one ever outgrows the need to depend on another human being. When immature dependency is either exacerbated or created by the traumatic situation, as in the case of Eva and Sam, it thwarts integration, growth, robs relational vitality and hope, and undermines the chances for improvement in mutual coping.

Transference exploration and analyses were used with Eva and Sam to help repair damaged internalized images and related mental structures linked to violent assault and cultural abandonment and neglect. Therapists are often tested in terms of their own potential to act on violent thoughts and impulses, and their attitudes toward victims and perpetrators of violence. The view here is that the therapist who is not clear on these issues would find it inordinately difficult to assist the couple, especially Eva in identifying, clarifying, analyzing, and mastering the internalized image and control of a violent offender.

The relational aspects deepen in this phase, though their importance traverses the entire therapy process, beginning in the assessment phase, continuing throughout the entire InTCT process. Relational factors are critical in restructuring image, cognition, affects, and behavior related to the couple's traumas (Brown, Scheflin, & Hammond, 1998; Parson, 1997a, 1997b, 1998a, 1998b, 1999).

Evaluation of Intertrauma Couples Therapy

The InCTC model includes assessment/diagnosis, treatment, and evaluation. Evaluation is essential because it informs when to shift and adjust the focus of treatment, modify intensity in certain areas, increase intensity in others, and when to terminate. A number of widely used instruments for couples in therapy may be used since they are sensitive to short-term changes. Initial results of an evaluation may show that partners' functioning and relationship is deteriorating. Eva and Sam were informed that things may get worse before they get better. This is expected because treatment revives long-term emotional pain and anguish, anger, heightened anxiety, depressive affect, distrust, and relationship-subverting dissociative defenses.

PHASE 5.
POST-INTEGRATION
AND AUTONOMOUS LIFE SKILLS PRACTICE

Intertrauma couple therapy ends with an integrated post-therapy plan that ensures the gains acquired by the couple continue *for life.* The dynamics, development, and maintenance of hope represent the engine that drives change when the couple attain agentic control and responsibility in pursuing goals and forging pathways for a positive life of engagement and fulfillment (Kwon, 2000; Parson, 1998a), and prevention of relapse in transactional functioning. Phase 5 is characterized by the couple's improved capacity for executive cognitive functioning (ECF; Giancola, Zeichner, Yarnell, & Dickson, 1996). ECF refers to the couple's capacity for strategic planning, abstract reasoning, attentional control, taking initiative, and an integrated, working memory.

After the formal elements of intertrauma couple therapy have come to an end, the post-treatment elements begin. The couple now embarks on a special system of post-treatment activity this writer calls the *autonomous life skills practice* (LSP; Parson, 1997c). This autonomous practice is a systematic, highly personalized plan of action developed with the couple to be implemented on a daily basis after termination of treatment. The concept derives from this writer's clinical experience of over 20 years of observation of the course of trauma illness in children, men, women, military, and civilian populations in America and in war-torn areas of the world. This experience has led to the conclusion that contemporary treatment for trauma patients often lacks long-term resolution, failing to recognize the vulnerabilities that continue far beyond termination phase of the treatment. It is clear that therapeutic gains attained by a victim/survivor in traumacare are often fleeting, with basic failure in post-therapeutic maintenance.

LSP is designed to give the person a sense of *integrative mastery* and developmental well-being. Like psychopharmacologic agents which regulate mood and behavior by impacting underlying biochemistry, LSP is a post-treatment strategy to regulate thought, mood, and behavior by persistent practice. Unlike drug therapy, however, LSP is insight- and skills-based founded upon learnings acquired during the course of trauma psychotherapy.

The practice procedures are geared to create a *psychological immune system* for the couple. This system prevents the irritability, negative mood and attitude changes that damage the marriage relationship. LSP thus teaches the couple how to conduct ongoing relational risk management through risk assessments, and maintenance of honesty in the relationship and reaching out to others. The couple's quality of life (Mendlowicz & Stein, 2000) is preeminent during this period of growth and forward movement. Resolving and managing the individuality-relatedness dialectic (Guisinger & Blatt, 1994) proved a major challenge for Sam and Eva. Emphasizing individuality, identity, and independence was tempered by a matured perspective of interdependence and connection.

The practice (LSP) helps the PTSD couple develop a strategy to stay well and prevent breakdown of intimacy, forestall post-traumatic decline, and the revival of anger and hostility, and relationship-subverting trauma-based defensiveness (for example, avoidance, dissociative symptoms, impulsivity, etc.). Part of the overall strategy involves how to respond before, during, and after a stressful event occurs. First, they ponder the who, what, where, and when questions, and then take skills-based action to change the situation.

LSP employs many principles identified in Meichenbaum's (1986,

1994) "stress inoculation training" and Snaith's (1998) "Anxiety Control Training."

This program also required Eva and Sam to engage continually in victims assistance programs, reaching out to make friends, taking vacations, going on picnics, taking a cruise, and doing other "fun activities" together. These activities are new for this couple: They had never done any of them before the treatment.

THERAPIST'S FUNCTIONS:
A SELF SYSTEMS/COUPLE SYSTEMS STRATEGIST

What an intertraumatically-disturbed couple needs in order to overcome the impact of trauma is the presence of a person who can "be blindly trusted when one's own resources are inadequate" (van der Kolk, 1987b, p. 32). The therapist's personality and "skilled work ego" are intrinsic aspects of intertrauma couples treatment. From the technical point of view, doing couple traumatherapy requires a therapist with experience in the fields of psychotherapy, couple therapy, and in traumatic stress (additional therapist qualifications are mentioned in a later section). Additionally, therapists understand that a focus on emotions should not be neglected in treatment, but that the ebb and flow of emotional dramas in treatment of clinical experience (LeDoux, 1996; Piercy, Lipschik, & Kiser, 2000).

Essentially, the therapist, as a self systems/couple systems strategist, interrupts the chaotic, dissociative homeostasis of the trauma cycle that maintains the cardinal symptoms of PTSD and dissociation. The therapist also understands the pervasive effects and persistence of traumatic distress, dissociative symptoms, depression, anxiety, and substance abuse and other comorbidities often associated with chronic PTSD and dissociation. Additionally, the therapist is comfortable with *reading defenses.* Defense-reading gives the therapist an important edge to help the couple arrive at the truth of their lives and forge a path to recovery and integration (Birmes et al., 2000; Kwon, 2000). The therapist does not ignore transcultural factors in therapy (Celano & Kaslow, 2000; Kaslow, Celano, & Dreelin, 1995; Lee, 1994; Miller, 1999; Sue, 1990), and is aware of the possible role of shame, self-blame, guilt, and fear of death play in the transactions of couples.

In treating Eva and Sam, it was necessary for the therapist to understand the impact and course of traumatic burn–dissociative symptoms, loss of trust, depression and anxiety, anger against the technological system that produced the disaster (in Sam's case, his anger was directed against the corporation and its leadership whom he perceived as uncaring and non-supportive). Naturally, both partners shared a variety of symptoms, though their expressions varied in the treatment and in the relationship.

It is also very important that therapists know how to establish an intertrauma couple treatment plan. The attainment of personal maturity in self-knowledge and self-control over emotional reactivity in the therapy is critical. This is especially relevant when the therapist's "personal buttons are pushed," especially if the therapist is a victim/survivor. The importance of therapist maturity and control may not come into play in most behavioral and some cognitive treatment procedures. However, when relational factors are explored and processed interpersonal dimensions of the trauma will revive with intensity issues as intimacy, betrayal, trust, dependency, love, hate, and narcissistic injury and rage.

Maturity and a secure identity are also required when, in couple's therapy, gender politics with its inherent emotional intensities and reality-distorting influence enter the clinical picture. The need to confront one's own sense of vulnerability to catastrophe, and fear induced by the couple's emotional intensity, is imperative. For an intertrauma couple transformation and change can occur only as the therapist challenges the couple to change, in part by offering them meaningful and workable alternatives to trauma thinking, feeling, and behaving. He/she also knows the dynamics of hope (Kwon, 2000).

In sum, the healing, integrative role of the therapist is: (1) knowledge of trauma theory, trauma pathology, and health, achieving mastery of change processes and techniques (to include assessment and diagnosis, and treatment of traumatic illness, learning problems, memory disturbance, self-other aggression, psychosomatic responses, and judicious decision to medical consultations for psychopharmacologic agents), in treating traumatized persons in individual, couple, and group modalities; (2) assess comorbidity issues (for Eva and Sam, substance abuse, depression, and PTSD), developmental physical and sexual abuse, neglect, understanding that the couple's treatment is not limited to the traumagenic events; (3) promote regulation physiological arousal, while maintaining stability and protection against intrusive ideation, painful mood, and internally fragmenting anxiety; (4) repair the couple's attachment capability devastated by negative, explosive transactions, taking into account the partners' post-trauma personality traits; (5) use countertransference responses to enhance the treatment (Parson, 1994b; Wilson & Lindy, 1994), (6) recognize the salutary aspects of the couple's trauma; and (7) employ Autonomous Life Skills Practice for long-term resolution and control over trauma-disrupting mental and behavioral sequelae.

On a symbolic note, this author sees the *critical presence* and functions of the trauma couple therapist as analogous to the New York City subway system's third rail. While travelers on the subway train are supported by two main rails (or tracks), the third rail gives both direction and an energizing function to ensure progress and positive movement forward to a predetermined destination. It's the job of the main rails to carry to do the work, to carry the load and take responsibility for the enterprise. The third rail offers an invaluable guaranteeing assistance for goals-fulfillment.

CONCLUSIONS

The focus of this contribution was on the assessment and treatment of couples with a collective personal history of *multiple* traumatic experiences. Trauma truly confronts people's sense of existential helplessness and vulnerability, altering basic biological, psychological, and social functions. The traumatic experiences shared by the intertrauma couple is a part of their lives. Therapy helps them to sort out what happened and address what happened–together. Putting the emotions and trauma-based ideas into words transforms fear into control with the aid of direct therapeutic exposing techniques and relational explorations.

A new treatment model, the *intertrauma couples therapy,* was presented to offer a comprehensive, multiphasic, and multitheoretical framework for traumatized couples. This article was written to highlight the special problems of the multiply traumatized couple in which both are victim/survivors of overwhelming events such as rape, war, disasters, and criminal assault. The position here is that, despite the positive benefits of talking, talking is *not* enough (Parson, 1984). There is the need "to take some action that symbolizes triumph over helplessness and despair" (van der Kolk, McFarlane, & Waisaeth, 1996). In intertrauma couples therapy "to take some action" with Eva and Sam began with (1) the couple's decision to come to therapy in the first place and going through the assessment process, (2) "hanging-in" through the treatment experience and not giving up the countless times when things became tough, (3) following through on homework assignments when the partners did not want to do so, (4) the specific cognitive and behavioral/actional procedures required of the couple during the course of the treatment (which included "going on dates," getting involved in volunteering at organizations that assist trauma victims), and (5) continuing post-treatment with the life-skills practice training.

This treatment model may be extended to meet the post-trauma needs of multiply traumatized families in search for integration and wholeness after overwhelming events. The model presented in this article offers a perspective that may be applied to interventions in societal and international trauma in which family members are traumatized either alone or together. Future research into the efficacy of intertraumatic couples therapy is indispensable for determining efficacy and generalizability.

REFERENCES

Allen, J., & Smith, W. (1995). *Diagnosis and treatment of dissociative disorders.* Northvale, NJ: Aronson.

American Psychiatric Association (1994). *Diagnostic and statistical manual of mental disorders.* Washington, DC: American Psychiatric Association.

Amir, N., Stafford, J., Freshman, M., & Foa, E. (1998). Relationship between narratives and trauma pathology. *Journal of Traumatic Stress, 11,* 385-392.

Anderson, J. (1995). *Learning and memory: An integrated approach.* New York: Wiley.

Arata, C., Picou, J., Johnson, D., & McNally, T. (2000). Coping with technological disaster: An application of the Conservation of Resource Model to the *Exxon Valdez* oil spill. *Journal of Traumatic Stress, 13,* 23-40.

Becker-Lausen, E., Sanders, B., & Chinsky, J. (1995). Meditation of abusive childhood experiences: Depression, dissociation, and negative life outcomes. *American Journal of Orthopsychiatry, 65,* 560-565.

Bergner, R. (2000). Love and barriers to love: An analysis for psychotherapists and others. *American Journal of Psychotherapy, 54,* 1-18.

Birmes, P., Warner, B., Callahan, S., Sztulman, H., Charlet, J., & Schmitt, L. (2000). Defense styles and post-traumatic stress disorder. *Journal of Nervous and Mental Disease, 188,* 306-308.

Boszormenyi-Nagy, I., & Spark, G. (1973). *Invisible loyalties: Reciprocity in intergenerational family therapy.* New York: Brunner/Mazel.

Bowlby, J. (1969). *Attachment and loss: Vol. 1. Attachment.* New York: Basic Books.

Bowlby, J. (1977). *The making and breaking of affectional bonds.* London: Tavistock.

Brown, D., Scheflin, A., & Hammond, C. (1998). *Memory, trauma treatment and the law: An essential reference on memory for clinicians, researchers, attorneys, and judges.* New York: Norton.

Brodsky, B., Cloitre, M., & Dulit, R. (1995). Relationship of dissociation to self-mutilation and childhood abuse in borderline personality disorder. *American Journal of Psychiatry, 152,* 1788-1792.

Cardeña, E., & Spiegel, D. (1993). Dissociative reactions to the Bay Area earthquake. *American Journal of Psychiatry, 150,* 474-478.

Carlson, E. (1997). *Trauma assessments: A clinician's guide.* New York: Guilford Press.

Carlson, E., & Putnam, F. (1993). An update on the Dissociative Experience Scale. *Dissociation, 6,* 16-27.

Celano, M., & Kaslow, N. (2000). Culturally competent family intervention; Review and case illustrations. *American Journal of Family Therapy, 28,* 217.

Coleman, S., Fanelli, A., & Gedeon, S. (2000). Psychology of the scientist: LXXXIL. Coverage of classical conditioning in textbooks in the psychology of learning. *Psychological Reports, 86,* 1011-1027.

Collins, N., & Feeney, B. (2000). A safe haven: An attachment theory perspective on support seeking and caregiving in intimate relationships. *Journal of Personality and Social Psychology, 78,* 1053-1073.

Compton, J., & Follette, V. (1998). Couples surviving trauma: Issues and interventions. In V. Follette, J. Ruzek, & F. Abueg (Eds.), *Cognitive-behavioral therapies for trauma* (pp. 321-352). New York: Guilford Press.

Dancu, C., Riggs, Hearst-Ikeda, D., Shoyer, B., & Foa, E. (1996). Dissociative experiences and PTSD among female victims of criminal assault and rape. *Journal of Traumatic Stress, 9I,* 253-267.

Dutton, M. (1998). Trauma assessments. *Centering, 3,* 1-8.

Everly, G. (1993). Neurophysiological considerations in the treatment of PTSD: A neurocognitive perspective. In J. Wilson & B. Raphael (Eds.), *International handbook of traumatic stress syndromes.* (795-802). New York: Plenum Publishing Corporation.

Field, T. (1985). Attachment as a psychobiological attunement: Being on the same wavelength. In M. Reite and T. Field (Eds.), *The psychobiology of attachment and separation.* Ireland, Florida: Academic Press.

Figley, C., & McCubbin, H. (1983). *Stress and the Family, Volume II: Coping with catastrophe.* New York: Brunner/Mazel.

Figley, C. (1994). Systemic post-traumatic stress disorder. Family treatment experiences and implications. In G. Everly & J. Lating (Eds.), *Post-traumatic stress.* New York: Plenum Press.

Foa, E., & Tolin, D. (2000). Comparison of the PTSD Symptom Scale–Interview Version and the Clinician-Administered PTSD Scale. *Journal of Traumatic Stress, 13,* 181-192.

Foa, E., Riggs, D., Dancu, C., & Rothbaum, B. (1993). Reliability and validity of a brief instrument for assessing post-traumatic stress disorder. *Journal of Traumatic Stress, 6,* 459-474.

Foa, E., & Rothbaum, B. (1998). *Treating the trauma of rape: Cognitive-behavioral therapy for PTSD.* New York: Guilford.

Follette, V., Ruzek, J., & Abueg, F. (1998). *Cognitive-behavioral therapies for trauma.* New York: Guilford Press.

Follingstad, D., & DeHart, D. (2000). Defining psychological abuse of husbands toward wives. *Journal of Interpersonal Violence, 15,* 891-920.

Frederick, C. (1985). Children traumatized by catastrophic situations. In S. Eth and R. Pynoos (Eds.), *Post-traumatic stress disorder in children.* Washington, DC: American Psychiatric Press.

Freud, S. (1920). Beyond the pleasure principle. *Standard Edition, 18,* 3-64.

Friedman, M. (2000). A guide to the literature on pharmacotherapy for PTSD. *PTSD Research Quarterly, 11,* 1-8.

Furst, S. (1967). *Psychic trauma.* New York: Basic Books.

Giancola, P., Zeichner, A., Yarnell, J., & Dickson, K. (1996). Relation between executive cognitive functioning and the adverse consequences of alcohol use in social drinkers. *Alcoholism: Clinical and experimental research, 20,* 1094-1098.

Gil, E. (1991). *The healing power of play: Working with abused children.* New York: The Guilford Press.

Green, B., Goodman, L., Krupnick, J., Corcoran, C., Petty, R., Stockton, P. & Stern, N. (2000). Outcomes of single versus multiple trauma exposure in a screening sample. *Journal of Traumatic Stress, 13,* 271-286.

Griffiths, M. (1997). Psychology of computer use: Some comments on "addictive use of the internet" by the young. *Psychological Reports, 80,* 81-82.

Grotstein, J. (1981). *Splitting and projective identification.* New York: Aronson.

Herman, J. (1992). *Trauma and recovery.* New York: Basic Books.

Holmes, J. (1993). Attachment theory: A biological basis for psychotherapy? *British Journal of Psychiatry, 163,* 430-438.

Horowitz, M. (1986). *Stress response syndromes.* (2nd Edition). Northvale, NJ: Aronson.

Hyer, L., Albrecht, W., Boudewyns, P., Woods, M., & Brandsma, J. (1993). Dissociative experienced in Vietnam veterans with chronic post-traumatic stress disorder. *Psychological Reports, 73,* 519-530.

Jacobson, N., & Christensen, A. (1996). *Integrative couple therapy: Promoting acceptance and change.* New York: Norton.

Janet, P. (1907). *The major symptoms of hysteria: Fifteen lectures given in the medical school of Harvard University.* New York: Macmillan.

Kaslow, N., Loundy, M., & Wood, K. (1998). A cultural perspective on families across the life cycle: Family patterns, assessment, and intervention. *Comprehensive clinical psychology* (172-205). New York: Pergamon.

Keane, T., Zimmering, R., & Caddell, J. (1985). A behavioral formulation of post-traumatic stress disorder in Vietnam veterans. *Behavior Therapy, 8,* 9-12.

Kilpatrick, D., Veronen, L., & Resnick, P. (1979). The aftermath of rape: Recent empirical findings. *American Journal of Orthopsychiatry, 49,* 658-659.

Kimmerling, R.l, Clum, G., & Wolfe, J. (2000). Relationship among trauma exposure, chronic post-traumatic stress disorder symptoms, and self-reported health in women: Replication and extension. *Journal of Traumatic Stress, 13,* 115-128.

Kirschner, S., & Kirschner, D. (1993). Couples and families. In G. Stricker & J. Gold (Eds.), *Comprehensive handbook of psychotherapy integration* (pp. 401-412).

Kluft, R. (1990). Editorial: The darker side of dissociation. *Dissociation, 3,* 125.

Koch, E. (2000). Representations of dread: The dreaded self and the dreaded state of the self. *Psychoanalytic Quarterly, 69,* 289-316.

Kohut, H. (1977). *The restoration of the self.* New York: International Universities Press.

Kolb, L. (1987). A neurophysiological hypothesis explaining post-traumatic stress disorders. *American Journal of Psychiatry, 1144,* 989-995.

Kolb, L. (1993). The psychobiology of PTSD: Perspectives and reflections on the past, present and future. *Journal of Traumatic Stress, 6,* 293-304. In J. Wilson and J. Lindy (Eds.), *Countertransference in the treatment of post-traumatic stress disorder* (pp. 151-178). New York: Guilford.

Kraemer, G. (1992). A psychobiological theory of attachment. *Behavioral and brain sciences, 15,* 493-541.

Kwon, P. (2000). Hope and dysphoria: The moderating role of defense. *Journal of Personality, 68,* 199-223.

Lambourn-Kavcic, B., & Day, H. (1995). Characteristics of male partners of adult female incest survivors. *Journal of Contemporary Psychotherapy, 25,* 387-398.

Le Doux, J. (1996). *The emotional brain: The mysterious underpinnings of emotional life.* New York: Simon & Schuster.

Lee, Y. (1994). Why does American psychology have cultural limitations? *American Psychologist, 55,* 524-525.

Levy, M. (2000). A conceptualization of the repetition compulsion. *Psychiatry, 63,* 45-52.

Loring, M. (1994). *Emotional abuse.* New York: Lexington.

Maltas, C., & Shay, J. (1995). Trauma contagious in partners of survivors of childhood sexual abuse. *American Journal of Orthopsychiatry, 65,* 529-539.

Marks, I., & Dar, R. (2000). Fear reduction by psychotherapies: Recent findings, future directions. *British Journal of Psychiatry, 176,* 512-513.

Marmar, C., Foy, D., Kagan, B., & Pynoos, R. (1994). An integrated approach to treating post-traumatic stress. In R. Pynoos (Ed.), *Post-traumatic stress disorder: A clinical review.* Lutherville, MD: Sidran Press.

Marmar, C., Weiss, D., Schlenger, W., Fairbank, J., Jordan, B., Kilka, R. & Hough, R. (1994). Peritraumaticdissociation and post-traumatic stress in male Vietnam theater veterans. *American Journal of Psychiatry, 151,* 902-907.

Matsakis, A. (1989a). Dual trauma couples. *Vet Center Voice, 10(6),* 3-5.

Matsakis, A. (1989b). Triple and quadruple trauma couples. *Vet Center Voice, 10(7),* 11-13.

Matsakis, A. (1994), Dual, triple, and quadruple trauma couples: Dynamics and treatment issues. In M. B. Williams & J. F. Sommers (Eds.), *Handbook of post-traumatic therapy* (pp. 78-93). Westport, CT: Greenwood.

Matsakis, A. (1996). *Vietnam wives: Facing the challenges of life with veterans suffering post-traumatic stress.* Lutherville, MD: Sidran Press.

Matsakis, A. (2000). *Emotional claustrophobia.* Oakland, CA: New Harbinger Publications.

Meichenbaum, D. H. (1986). *Stress inoculation training.* New York: Pergamon.

Meichenbaum, D. (1994). *A clinical handbook/practical therapist manual: For assessing and treating adults with post-traumatic stress disorder (PTSD).* Waterloo, Ontario: Institute Press.

Mendlowicz, M., & Stein, M. (2000). Quality of the life in individuals with anxiety disorders. *American Journal of Psychiatry, 157,* 669-682.

Miller, J. (1999). Cultural psychology: Implications for basic psychological theory. *Psychological Science, 10,* 85-91.

Minuchin, S. (1996). *Mastering family therapy: Journeys of growth and transformation.* New York: Wiley.

Nichols, W. (1998). Integrative marital therapy. In F. Dattilio (Ed.), *Case studies in couple and family therapy: Systemic and cognitive perspectives* (pp. 233-256). New York: Guilford Press.

Nickerson, R. (1999). How we know–and sometimes misjudge–what others know: Imputing one's own knowledge to others. *Psychological Bulletin, 125,* 737-759.

Norcross, J., & Goldfried, M. (1992). *Handbook of psychotherapy integration.* New York: Basic Books.

Parson, E. (1984). The reparation of the self. *Journal of Contemporary Psychotherapy, 14,* 4-54.

Parson, E. R. (1988). Post-traumatic self disorders. In J. Wilson, Z. Harel, & B. Kahana (Eds.), *Human adaptation to extreme stress: From the Holocaust to Vietnam.* Plenum.

Parson, E. (1994a). Post-traumatic Stress Disorder: Its Biopsychobehavioral Aspects and Management. In B. Wolman & G. Stricker (Eds.), *Anxiety and Anxiety-Related Disorders* (pp. 226-385). New York: Wiley.

Parson, E. (1994b). Inner City Children of Trauma: Urban Violence Traumatic Stress Response Syndrome (U-VTS) and Therapists' Responses. In J. Wilson & J. Lindy (Eds.), *Countertransference in the treatment of post-traumatic stress disorder* (pp. 151-178). New York: Guilford.

Parson, E. (1995a). Post-traumatic stress and coping in an inner-city child: Traumatogenic witnessing of interparental violence and murder. *The Psychoanalytic Study of the Child, 50,* 272-307.

Parson, E. R. (1995b). Mass traumatic terror in Oklahoma City and the phases of adaptational coping, Part I: Possible effects of intentional injury/harm on victim's post-traumatic responses. *Journal of Contemporary Psychotherapy, 25,* 155-184.

Parson, E. R. (1995c). Mass traumatic terror in Oklahoma City and the phases of adaptational coping, Part II: Integration of cognitive, behavioral, dynamic, existential, and pharmacologic interventions. *Journal of Contemporary Psychotherapy, 25,* 267-309.

Parson, E. (1996a). Child Traumatherapy and the effects of trauma, loss, and dissociation: A multisystems approach to healing children exposed to lethal urban community violence. *Journal of Contemporary Psychotherapy, 26,* 117-162.

Parson, E. R. (1996a). Post-traumatic stress disorder. In B. Wolman (Ed.), *The Ency-*

clopedia of Psychiatry, Psychology and Psychoanalysis (pp. 406-412). New York: Henry Holt Company.

Parson, E. R. (1996b). "It Takes a Village to Heal a Child": Necessary Spectrum of Expertise and Benevolence by Therapists, Non-Governmental Organizations, and the United Nations in Managing War-Zone Stress in Children Traumatized by Political Violence. *Journal of Contemporary Psychotherapy, 26,* 251-286.

Parson, E. R. (1996c, March). *Trauma and dissociogenic functional impairments: Cognitive miscalculations and affective misalignments in victims of physical and sexual violence.* A Masters Class conducted at the Second Annual Conference on Trauma, Loss, and Dissociation: Foundations of 21st Century Traumatology, Georgetown University Medical Center and Kairos Ventures II, Ltd.

Parson, E. R. (1997). Post-traumatic child therapy (P-TCT): Assessment and treatment factors in clinical work with inner-city children exposed to catastrophic community violence. *Journal of Interpersonal Violence, 12,* 172-194.

Parson, E. R. (1997a). Traumatic stress personality disorder (TrSPD): Intertheoretical therapy for the PTSD/PD comorbid dissociogenic organization. *Journal of Contemporary Psychotherapy, 27,* 323-367.

Parson, E. R. (1997b). Post-Traumatic Child Therapy (P-TCT): Assessment and Treatment Factors in Clinical Work with Inner City Children Exposed to Catastrophic Community Violence. *Journal of Interpersonal Violence, 12,* 172-194.

Parson, E. R. (1997c). *Autonomous life skills practice and traumatherapy: Preventing eruption of violent impulses.* Paper presented at VA/Harvard Conference on Violence and Prevention, VA Headquarters, Washington, DC.

Parson, E. R. (1998a). Traumatherapy 2001, Part I: *"The Reparation of the Self"* Revisited on the Way Into the 21st Century. *Journal of Contemporary Psychotherapy, 28,* 239-275.

Parson, E. R. (1998b). Traumatherapy 2001, Part II: Traumatic stress personality disorder (TrSPD), Part II: Trauma assessment using the Rorschach and self-report tests. *Journal of Contemporary Psychotherapy, 28,* 45-68.

Parson, E. R. (1998c). Traumatic stress personality disorder (TrSPD), Part III: Mental/physical trauma representations–From focus on PTSD symptoms to inquiry into who the victim has now become. Journal of Contemporary Psychotherapy, 28, 141-172.

Parson, E. R. (1999). The voice in dissociation: A group model for helping victims integrate trauma representational memory. *Journal of Contemporary Psychotherapy, 29,* 19-38.

Piercy, F., Lipchik, E., & Kiser, D. (2000). Miller and de Shazer's article on "emotions in Solution-Focused Therapy." *Family Process, 39,* 25-28.

Proshaska, J. & Clement, C. (1982). Transtheoretical therapy: Toward a more integrative model of change: *Psychotherapy: Theory, Research, & Practice, 19,* 276-288.

Rabin, C., & Nardi, C. (1991). Treating post-traumatic stress disorder couples: A psychoeducational program. *Community Mental Health Journal, 27,* 209-224.

Resnick, H. (1996). Psychometric Review of Trauma Assessment for Adults (TAA). In B. H. Stamm, (Ed.), *Measurement of stress, trauma, and adaptation* (pp. 362-365). Lutherville, MD: Sidran Press.

Rutan, J., & Smith, J. (1985). Building therapeutic relationship with couples. *Psychotherapy, 22,* 194-200.

Salter, A. (1995). *Transforming trauma: A guide to understanding and treating adult survivors of child sexual abuse.* Thousand Oaks, CA: Sage.

Sanders, B., & Giolas, M. (1991). Dissociation and childhood trauma in psychologically disturbed adolescents. *American Journal of Psychiatry, 42,* 297-301.

Saxe, G., van der Kilk, B., Berkowitz, R., Chinman, G., Hall, K., Lieberg, G., & Schwartz, J. (1993). Dissociative disorders in psychiatric inpatients. *American Journal of Psychiatry, 150,* 1037-1042.

Schnurr, P., & Spiro, A. (1999). Combat exposure, post-traumatic stress disorder symptoms, and health behaviors as predictors of self-reported physical health in older veterans. *Journal of Nervous and Mental Disease, 187,* 353-359.

Schwartz, E., & Kowalski, J. (1993). Personality characteristics and post-traumatic stress symptoms after a school shooting. *Journal of Nervous and Mental Disease, 181,* 735-737.

Shaffer, H., Hall, M., & Vander Bilt, J. (2000). "Computer addiction": A critical consideration. *American Journal of Orthopsychiatry, 70,* 162-168.

Shapiro, F., & Forrest, M. (1997). *EMDR: The breakthrough therapy for overcoming anxiety, stress, and trauma.* New York: Basic Books.

Shelton, J., & Levy, R. (1981). *Behavioral assignments and treatment compliance: A handbook of clinical strategies.* Champaign, IL: Research Press.

Snaith, R. (1998). Meditation and psychotherapy. *British Journal of Psychiatry, 173,* 193-195.

Spasojevic, J., Heffer, R., & Snyder, D. (2000). Effects of post-traumatic stress and acculturation on marital functioning in Bosnian refugee couples. *Journal of Traumatic Stress, 13,* 205-217.

Spiegel, D. (1991). Forward. In A. Tasman & S. Goldfinger (Eds.), *American Psychiatric Press Review of Psychiatry* (Vol. 10, pp. 143-144). Washington, DC: American Psychiatric Press.

Steinberg, M. (1995). *Handbook for the assessment of dissociation: A clinical guide.* Washington, DC: American Psychiatric Press.

Sue, D. (1990). *Counseling the culturally different.* New York: Wiley & Sons.

Turkus, J. (1998). Trauma: The mind/body connection. *Centering, 3,* 1-6.

Ulman, R. & Brothers, J. (1989). *The shattered self.* Hillsdale, NJ: The Analytic Press.

van der Kolk, B. (1987a). The role of the group in trauma response. In *Psychological trauma* (pp. 153-171). Washington, DC: American Psychiatric Press.

van der Kolk, B. (1987b). The separation cry and the trauma response: Developmental issues in the psychobiology of attachment and response. In *Psychological trauma* (pp. 31-52). Washington, DC: American Psychiatric Press.

van der Kolk, B. (1996). The body keeps the score: Approaches to the psychobiology of post-traumatic stress disorder. In B. van der Kolk, A. McFarlane, & L. Weisaeth (Eds.), *Traumatic stress: The effects of overwhelming experience on mind, body, and society* (pp. 214-241). New York: Guilford.

Vivian, D., & Langhinsrichsen-Rohling, J. (1994). Are bi-directionally violent couples mutually victimized? A gender-sensitive comparison. *Violence and victims, 9,* 107-124.

Wagner, A., Wolfe, J., Rotnitsky, A., Proctor, S., & Erickson, D. (2000). An investigation of the impact of post-traumatic stress disorder on physical health. *Journal of Traumatic Stress, 13,* 41-56.

Weber, S. (2000). *The legend of Freud: Cultural memory in the present.* CA: Stanford University Press.

Wijma, K., Soderquist, J., Bjorklunk, I., & Wijma, B. (2000). Prevalence of post-traumatic stress disorder among gynecological patients with a history of sexual and physical abuse. *Journal of Interpersonal Violence, 15,* 944-958.

Williams, M. B. (1992). A systems view of psychological trauma: Developing post-traumatic stress response paradigms. *Journal of Contemporary Psychotherapy, 22,* 89-105.

Wilson, J., & Lindy, J. (1994)(Eds.), *Countertransference in the treatment of post-traumatic stress disorder* (pp. 151-178). New York: Guilford.

Zlotnick, C., Shea, T., Pearlstein, T., Simpson, E., Costello, E., & Begin, A. (1996). The relationship between dissociative symptoms, alexithymia, impulsivity, sexual abuse, and self-mutilation, *Comprehensive Psychiatry, 37,* 12-16.

Index

Able, 20
Abuse
    in boot camp, 32
    child, male, 30-33. *See also* Male
        abuse, in childhood
    versus discipline, in men raising
        boys to become men, 60-62
    and feelings of worthlessness, 6
    male
        by female intimates, 41-57. *See*
          also Male abuse, by female
          intimates
        impact on intimate relationships,
          29–39. *See also* Male abuse,
          impact on intimate
          relationships
Acceptance, in intertrauma couples
    therapy, 95-96
Affective traumatic stress response, to
    intertrauma couples therapy,
    86
Anger, outbursts of, in intertrauma
    couples therapy, 88-89
Anger management, ineffective, as
    symbol of authority, 67
Anxiety
    double character of, in intertrauma
        couples therapy, 96
    as symbol of authority, 67-68
Anxiety Control Training, 102
Archer, J., 46,49,51,53
Associative attachment, 83
Attachment, dissociative, 74
Authority, symbols of, in men raising
    boys to become men, 65-66
Autonomous life skill practice, in
    intertrauma couples therapy,
    100-102
Avoidance, in intertrauma couples
    therapy, 88

Balcom, D., 16,19-20
Barcus, R., 15-16,17,19
Becker, 20
Behavioral memory system, 97
Behavioral responses, in intertrauma
    couples therapy, 90-91
Belt, as symbol of authority in, 65-66
Biebl, W., 20
Biological responses, in intertrauma
    couples therapy, 82-89
Biopsychobehavioral responses,
    recognition and assessment
    of, in intertrauma couples
    therapy, 81-82
Bitman, I., 47
Blaming, defined, 6-7
Bland, R., 47
Bloom, A.D., 9
Body systems, effect of intertrauma
    couples therapy on, 85-86
Boot camp, abuse in, 32
Bower, 97
Boy(s), men raising of, to become
    men, 59-68. *See also* Men
    raising boys to become men
Brinkerhoff, 47
Briquet, P., 84
Buttenheim, M., 21,202

Canadian Urban Victimization Survey
    (CUVS), 48
Canadian Violence Against Women
    Survey (VAWS), 48
Cazaneave, N.A., 45
Character building, in men raising
    boys to become men, 63-64
Child abuse, male, 30-33. *See also*
    Male abuse, in childhood
Cognitive stress response, in intertrauma
    couples therapy, 89